FASHION

Fashion

EXAMINING POP CULTURE

MONIKA BOLINO, Book Editor

Daniel Leone, President
Bonnie Szumski, Publisher
Scott Barbour, Managing Editor
James D. Torr, Series Editor

**GREENHAVEN
PRESS®**

THOMSON
™
GALE

San Diego • Detroit • New York • San Francisco • Cleveland
New Haven, Conn. • Waterville, Maine • London • Munich

LIBRARY OF CONGRESS CATALOGING-IN-PUBLICATION DATA

Fashion / by Monika Bolino, book editor.
  p. cm.—(Examining pop culture series)
  Includes bibliographical references and index.
  ISBN 0-7377-1062-4 (hard : alk. paper) — ISBN 0-7377-1061-6 (pbk. : alk. paper)
    1. Fashion—Social aspects. [1. Fashion—Social aspects. 2. Popular culture—
  History—20th century.] I. Title. II. Series: Examining pop culture.
  GT525 .B65   2003
  391—dc21   2001007288

Printed in the United States of America

CONTENTS

Barbie Dolls, is similar to adult fashion magazines such as *Vogue* in its content. The stories and advertisements in both magazines reinforce female stereotypes and promote an unrealistic feminine beauty ideal.

Chapter 2: Men's Attire as an Indicator of Social Class

Chapter 3: Fashion as a Business

"designer" clothes are no longer the domain of an elite circle of consumers. High fashion has become popularized, and it has suffered as a result.

Chapter 4: Fashion, Culture, and Controversy

FOREWORD

POPULAR CULTURE IS THE COMMON SET OF ARTS, entertainments, customs, beliefs, and values shared by large segments of society. Russel B. Nye, one of the founders of the study of popular culture, wrote that "not until the appearance of mass society in the eighteenth century could popular culture, as one now uses the term, be said to exist." According to Nye, the Industrial Revolution and the rise of democracy in the eighteenth and nineteenth centuries led to increased urbanization and the emergence of a powerful middle class. In nineteenth-century Europe and North America, these trends created audiences for the popular arts that were larger, more concentrated, and more well off than at any point in history. As a result, more people shared a common culture than ever before.

The technological advancements of the twentieth century vastly accelerated the spread of popular culture. With each new advance in mass communication—motion pictures, radio, television, and the Internet—popular culture has become an increasingly pervasive aspect of everyday life.

Popular entertainment—in the form of movies, television, theater, music recordings and concerts, books, magazines, sporting events, video games, restaurants, casinos, theme parks, and other attractions—is one very recognizable aspect of popular culture. In his 1999 book *The Entertainment Economy: How Mega-Media Forces Are Transforming Our Lives*, Michael J. Wolf argues that entertainment is becoming the dominant feature of American society: "In choosing where we buy French fries, how we relate to political candidates, what airline we want to fly, what pajamas we choose for our kids, and which mall we want to buy them in, entertainment is increasingly influencing every one of those choices. . . . Multiply that by the billions of choices that, collectively, all of us make each day and you have a portrait of a society in which entertainment is one of its leading institutions."

It is partly this pervasive quality of popular culture that makes it worthy of study. James Combs, the author of *Polpop: Politics and Popular Culture in America*, explains that examining

9

popular culture is important because it can shape people's attitudes and beliefs:

> Popular culture is so much a part of our lives that we cannot deny its developmental powers. . . . Like formal education or family rearing, popular culture is part of our "learning environment.". . . Though our pop culture education is informal—we usually do not attend to pop culture for its "educational" value—it nevertheless provides us with information and images upon which we develop our opinions and attitudes. We would not be what we are, nor would our society be quite the same, without the impact of popular culture.

Examining popular culture is also important because popular movies, music, fads, and the like often reflect popular opinions and attitudes. Christopher D. Geist and Jack Nachbar explain in *The Popular Culture Reader*, "the popular arts provide a gauge by which we can learn what Americans are thinking, their fears, fantasies, dreams, and dominant mythologies. The popular arts reflect the values of the multitude."

This two-way relationship between popular culture and society is evident in many modern discussions of popular culture. Does the glorification of guns by many rap artists, for example, merely reflect the realities of inner-city life, or does it also contribute to the problem of gun violence? Such questions also arise in discussions of the popular culture of the past. Did the Vietnam protest music of the late 1960s and early 1970s, for instance, simply reflect popular antiwar sentiments, or did it help turn public opinion against the war? Examining such questions is an important part of understanding history.

Greenhaven Press's *Examining Pop Culture* series provides students with the resources to begin exploring these questions. Each volume in the series focuses on a particular aspect of popular culture, with topics as varied as popular culture itself. Books in the series may focus on a particular genre, such as *Rap and Hip Hop*, while others may cover a specific medium, such as *Computers and the Internet*. Volumes such as *Body Piercing and Tattoos* have their focus on recent trends in popular culture, while titles like *Americans' Views About War* have a broader historical scope.

In each volume, an introductory essay provides a general

overview of the topic. The selections that follow offer a survey of critical thought about the subject. The readings in *Americans' Views About War*, for example, are arranged chronologically: Essays explore how popular films, songs, television programs, and even comic books both reflected and shaped public opinion about American wars from World War I through Vietnam. The essays in *Violence in Film and Television*, on the other hand, take a more varied approach: Some provide historical background, while others examine specific genres of violent film, such as horror, and still others discuss the current controversy surrounding the issue.

Each book in the series contains a comprehensive index to help readers quickly locate material of interest. Perhaps most importantly, each volume has an annotated bibliography to aid interested students in conducting further research on the topic. In today's culture, what is "popular" changes rapidly from year to year and even month to month. Those who study popular culture must constantly struggle to keep up. The volumes in Greenhaven's *Examining Pop Culture* series are intended to introduce readers to the major themes and issues associated with each topic, so they can begin examining for themselves what impact popular culture has on their own lives.

THE IMPORTANCE OF CLOTHING IN AMERICAN culture is wryly summarized by writer Mark Twain's observation, "Clothes make the man. Naked people have little or no influence on society." Twain's proverb acknowledges the link between fashion and personal identity. In modern America, clothes have become a complicated form of personal expression. Sociologist Alison Lurie notes that "even if we are never introduced, clothes tell about class status, age, family origin, personal opinion, taste, current mood or even give information about erotic interest and sexual status." In short, what a person wears indicates a great deal about who that person is, and who he or she wants to be.

In contrast to clothing, *fashion* refers to the styles of dress that are prevalent in society at any given time. In their book *Changing Appearances*, George B. Sproles and Leslie Davis Burns define fashion as "the style of a consumer product, the symbolic meaning attached to the product, or the process by which the product is adopted by individuals and social groups." In *Lead Us into Temptation*, cultural critic James Twitchell notes that virtually anything can fall in or out of "fashion," including soda, television programs, and home furnishings. Historian Gayle Fischer clarifies that fashion is "both a process and an end product."

Sproles and Burns maintain that the history of fashion in America is closely connected to the social history of the country as a whole. In the nineteenth century in particular, developments including frontier expansion, the advent of mass manufacturing technology, and the growth of cities resulted in profound changes in Americans' attitudes about work, home life, and recreation. These changing attitudes were reflected in nineteenth-century fashions.

Fashion and Gender Roles

American fashion has always been divided along gender lines, but Fischer notes that this division became especially clear in the nineteenth century. Nineteenth-century women were supposed to be demure, inactive, and tied to the house, while men typically spent their time outside the home at work. Fashion trends reflected these gender roles. Men's fashions became more functional, emphasizing "cut and fit above ornament, color, and display." Women's clothing, on the other hand, became more "flamboyant," characterized by exaggerated bustlines, hoop skirts, and corsets. Worn under clothing, corsets were tightly laced garments that cinched the torso into unhealthy proportions (cultural historian David Kunzle documents stories of women whose corsets gave them thirteen-inch waists).

Such garments made it difficult for women to move quickly or efficiently. Fischer notes that it was not uncommon for women to wear "as much as twenty-five or thirty-five yards of cloth just in the skirts." Any deviation from this dress code—even to perform household chores more easily—was considered unbecoming or even scandalous. Some women complained that long dresses and starched skirts were burdensome for their daily activities, but they remained bound by nineteenth-century morals to wear them.

By the end of the nineteenth century, many women had become annoyed with the impracticality of long skirts and corsets which restrained movement. They began calling for "dress reform." Dress reformers rallied for alternative garments such as shorter skirts, pants, and for the abandonment of the corset altogether. The women's campaign for dress reform coincided with the burgeoning women's rights movement. According to historian Jill Fields, "women's claims to wagework, to academic and physical education, to public protest over access to suffrage and birth control, and to pleasurable leisure activities such as dancing at tango parties all brought daily corset wearing into question."

The acceptance of women wearing pants remains one of American fashion's profound developments. When women first took to the streets in trousers in the nineteenth century, public outcries were heard throughout the United States. Until then pants were only worn in public by men, and strictly in private by women. But according to Fischer, pants had become unisex attire by the 1940s.

One event that helped pants gain acceptance across gender

Women in the nineteenth century dressed in corsets and large hoop skirts that often restricted their movements.

lines was the second world war. Fashion scholar Beverly Gordon observes that World War II provided an "excuse" for women to forego skirts and dresses in favor of work pants, particularly blue jeans, when they took over traditionally male jobs as American men were sent off to war. In one sense, wearing pants became a patriotic gesture; in another, wearing pants symbolized the movement of women from the home into the workforce. Nevertheless, pants are still associated with traditional male authority, as the familiar phrase "who wears the pants?" demonstrates.

More Fashion Choices for Men

Impractical clothing items such as the corset or high heels are often associated with women, but men also adhere to cultural fashion norms. The necktie is a prime example. Its nonfunctionality has been the subject of some ridicule—journalist Linda Ellerbee once joked, "If men can run the world, why can't they stop wearing neckties? How intelligent is it to start the day by tying a little noose around your neck?"—but neckties continue to be a symbol of power and masculinity in the American workforce.

The suit itself has a long history in America. Diana de Marly, in her study *Dress in North America: The New World, 1492–1800*, states that "the suit revolutionized male fashion," becoming the "male uniform." She notes the suit has changed surprisingly little in form from when it was first developed in the late 1670s.

As with women, more fashion options became available for men in the decades after World War II. In the 1960s, for example, longer hair came into style for both genders, partly due to the unprecedented popularity of British "long hair" bands such as the Beatles. The first men's fashion magazines were published at this time, as well, including *Gentleman's Quarterly* (later known simply as *GQ*). By the 1980s, men had more fashion choices than ever. Today, suits and button-down shirts remain the norm in the business world, but have been supplemented by more relaxed or active styles that often take their inspiration from sport culture.

Clothes and Personal Identity

In sharp contrast to previous eras, modern fashion is characterized primarily by individual choice. But with so many clothing styles now available, what determines a person's choice of dress? Why do people choose the fashions that they do? In the 1920s, Elizabeth Hurlock studied the psychological aspects of clothing, noting, "Today, there are no laws which make us accept a fashion. No fashion is imposed upon an individual by force." Social scientists Sproles and Burns agree that modern American "fashion is a personal choice," but suggest that individual fashion decisions are guided by external influences such as the media or popular opinion.

According to Sproles and Burns, fashion helps fulfill several human "social-psychological needs." First, people have a need to be "up-to-date," and to "adjust to a changing society." Sproles and Burns explain that in American culture, "it is considered socially desirable to be considered modern and new." Wearing the latest styles demonstrates that the wearer is a forward thinker. A related need is the "desire to escape boredom," which is satisfied by trying out the newest look.

Clothing can also help meet two other sociopsychological needs listed by Sproles and Burns—the "need for symbolic differentiation," and the "need for social affiliation." In this view, fashion is a way for people to express their uniqueness—to differentiate themselves from others—as well as a chance to demonstrate solidarity with—or affiliation to—similar groups and communities.

Fashion and Body Image

Clothing may boost one's confidence and sense of belonging, but some fashion trends have been charged with encouraging a negative self-image. Writing about the continuing popularity of ultra-thin supermodels, journalist Kate Betts observes, "Fashion, which can make people feel beautiful and glamorous, can also make people feel worse about themselves if they're not as beautiful, or as thin, or as fabulous as the swans in the pictures." Attitudes about body image have played a big part in shaping twentieth-century fashion. In *The Fashion Business: Theory, Practice, Image*, author Valerie Steele notes that in the 1980s, media images began to place a greater emphasis on physical fitness. A muscular and fit body was as much "in fashion" as the hippest clothing. Even the 1984 Barbie doll line embraced the "sculpted" body ideal—"Great Shape Barbie" was described in the catalog as "trim 'n terrific" with "trendy looking" clothes.

The fashion world's emphasis on thin and toned bodies has fueled Americans' preoccupation with body image. Fashion insider Digna Rodriguez-Poulton says children as young as five years old "are worrying about their abs, about having flat bellies so they can wear short tops and pants with a three-inch inseam." She says that while the girls are simply following the styles set by their favorite celebrities or peers, the danger is that these adults "don't understand the messages they're sending." Meanwhile, manufacturers spend considerable time and money attracting young shoppers due to the relatively new and profitable youth market. In 2000 alone, preteen sales were estimated at $155 billion.

"Street" Trends Become Mainstream

Critics charge that designers and the media have promoted thinness as "fashionable"; but fashion trends often originate not with designers but with less mainstream fads. In particular, adolescent lifestyles and fads are increasingly the inspiration for mainstream trends. Until the late 1950s, adolescents had dressed in smaller versions of adult styles; now, they often set the fashion agenda. According to Sproles and Burns, "young people favor innovation and change, making the youth culture a natural testing ground for new styles, and much of fashion merchandising is directed at youthful tastes."

One example is the "punk" movement in the mid-1970s. According to fashion historian Barbara Nordquist, the style is a classic example of how "streetwear" often becomes part of mainstream American fashion. Punk dress originated in Britain, where working class adolescents adopted an "anti-establishment" dress style to express their despair regarding economic and class issues. Cultural critic Dick Hebridge adds, "The punks wore clothes which were the . . . equivalent of swear words." One of the trademarks of punk fashion is the mockery of traditional dress by combining unexpected clothing items. Examples include wearing a tuxedo jacket with no shirt, or underwear as outerwear, or even wearing safety pins in unconventional ways—in place of zippers, or as body piercings, for instance. Hebridge describes the look as "'cheap' trashy fabrics (PVC, plastic, latex, etc.) in vulgar designs (e.g., mock leopard skin) and 'nasty' colors, long discarded by the quality end of the fashion industry as obsolete kitsch."

By the 1980s, punk represented both fashion and a lifestyle. According to Nordquist, punk dress has become a thriving business—one indication of its evolution from fad to fashion. Storeowners like Stephen Sprouse catered to consumers wanting the look. In 1987, Sprouse opened a three-level New York City boutique specializing in punk clothing— Day-Glo colors, miniskirts, motorcycle jackets—all still in demand, and priced for more mainstream consumers rather than the thrift store crowd. In the 1990s, Commander Salamander, a famous punk shop in Washington, D.C., sporting hot pink walls and "an eclectic mix of avant-garde and the shocking" continued to earn over a million dollars in sales each year. Furthermore, Nordquist points out, punk styles have blended into mainstream dress, with leather miniskirts and black clothing standard fare in department stores today.

Mass Media Influences on Individual Choice

Historians Patricia Cunningham and Susan Voso Lab agree that technology is also vital in passing along—and in some cases, such as women's pants, starting—trends. They note that "mass communication, which helps transmit the fashion message to large numbers of people, helps to promote fashion change." This new culture of "mass production" and quick communication has had a significant influence on how and why people select what they wear.

Author Grant McCracken suggests three ways that clothing is given meaning, and is therefore made desirable. According to McCracken, advertising, opinion leaders, and subculture groups are the three sources of fashion innovations. Subculture groups are groups "on the fringe of society," such as punks, hippies, or hip-hop enthusiasts. Advertising helps give value to goods, in the same way "opinion leaders"—such as movie stars, sports figures, and other celebrities—give value to styles and fads. One example is Spike Lee's baseball cap commemorating Malcolm X, a design which gained popularity after the director was photographed wearing it.

Indeed, fashion in the late twentieth century has become less focused on clothing designs themselves, and more preoccupied with logos and brands. According to James Twitchell, brand names have become a way for people to express their personal identity, or, in some cases, adopt a new one. Twitchell suggests that when customers purchase brand name fashions, they are not buying articles of clothing, but rather a personality or image. Ralph Lauren's "English colonial upper crust" look, for example, can be found on "sheets, shirts, shoes, sweatpants, sofas, [and] sunglasses." Twitchell describes one ad that epitomizes the identity of the Lauren line, and its wearers: "A two-page layout of the crushed white gravel in a driveway leading to a baronial estate. Nothing else is shown. You can almost hear the sound of your invisible Rolls-Royce as you motor up the driveway in your noveau, old-style Ralph Lauren outfit."

Fashion historian Lou Taylor believes that designer Tommy Hilfiger has become a leader of this new type of brand-name, advertising-driven fashion. Taylor writes, "Through expert marketing, Hilfiger has been able to market his mass-produced clothes as 'designer' products and even as high fashion." Hilfiger achieves this by using large designer strategies such as celebrity-filled runway shows, advertisements in "elite magazines," and marketing his line as a "lifestyle choice" for a young audience. As Taylor suggests, high status, high priced logos such as Lauren and Hilfiger are regarded as an investment as well as a way to identify with celebrity role models.

Individuality vs. Conformity

Thus, fashion today remains a contradiction. On the one hand, clothing is a way to express one's individual personality and philosophies. This is increasingly true as Americans become more tolerant of diversity and less constricted by dress codes in workplaces and schools. However, while consumers have more freedom to choose for themselves what to wear, their preferences are increasingly being guided—consciously and subconsciously—by the influence of mass media and mass marketing. Constant exposure to movies and television, music, professional sports, and other popular media impact Americans' fashion desires, and new technologies such as the Internet and cable television have caused trends and fads to be spread more quickly and broadly than ever before. American fashion has become an arena for the opposition between personal expression and imposed social norms. The articles in *Examining Pop Culture: Fashion* explore this tension and provide examples of how popular fashions reflect social, economic, and political aspects of American culture.

EXAMINING POP CULTURE

Women, Clothing, and Gender Roles

Women Wearing Pants: Dress Reform in the Nineteenth and Early Twentieth Centuries

Diana Crane

In nineteenth-century America, women were encouraged to wear skirts and dresses for all occasions—even household chores. Excessively tight waistlines and long, bulky skirts became especially popular, despite complaints that these styles were awkward and cumbersome. Some historians believe such fashion trends are clues to society's ideas about women's roles. For instance, women were regarded as less physically active than men and more suited for home-based pastimes. The impractical design of women's garments—which prevented physical movement—reflected this attitude.

In the mid-1850s, a movement called Alternative Dress Reform introduced more functional, or "rational," clothing for women, including three styles of pants. The movement corresponded to the rise of recreational and school sports such as bicycling, swimming, and horseback riding. These activities prompted women to leave the house and wear more

■

Excerpted from *Fashion and Its Social Agendas: Class, Gender, and Identity in Clothing*, by Diana Crane (Chicago: University of Chicago Press, 2000). Copyright © 2000 by The University of Chicago. Reprinted with permission.

comfortable, practical clothing. However, many Americans found these new styles shocking. Pants were scorned until the first half of the twentieth century when World War I material shortages and pants-wearing film actresses finally made it socially acceptable for women to wear unisex outfits. Author Diana Crane is a professor of sociology at the University of Pennsylvania. This article is excerpted from her book *Fashion and Its Social Agendas: Class, Gender, and Identity in Clothing*.

AT THE CENTER OF MUCH OF THE DEBATE ABOUT women's clothing in the nineteenth century were members of women's movements who attempted to bring about dress reform in the direction of practical, healthy, and comfortable clothing. They deplored the use of corsets and excessively heavy sets of garments . . . and centered their proposals on the adoption of trousers.

Trousers were particularly controversial in the nineteenth century, because nineteenth-century ideology prescribed fixed gender identities, enormous differences—physical, psychological, and intellectual—between men and women. The dominant point of view allowed for no ambiguity about sexual identification and no possibility for evolution or change in the prescribed behaviors and attitudes of members of each gender. Throughout the second half of the nineteenth century, dress reforms proposed by women's movements were inconsistent with this point of view and, consequently, were unable to win the support of substantial numbers of women outside these groups.

The Bloomer Costume

The first and best-known proposal for dress reform was also the most notorious—the costume proposed by Mrs. Amelia Bloomer in America in the 1850s—because it subverted gender differences. This costume consisted of a short skirt over a pair of full Turkish trousers. Bloomer, a women's activist, and a few of her fellow activists wore the costume because it was "comfortable, convenient, safe and tidy—with no thought of introducing a fashion." The enormous amount of attention and controversy the costume generated points to the salience of gender differentiation. When Bloomer, who published a women's temperance magazine, wrote an article in 1851 describing her new costume, the information was reprinted in a leading New York newspaper and subsequently in newspapers all over the country and abroad. Numerous articles described the costume's appearance in different cities and at various types of social events. It was said to be spreading throughout the nation "like wildfire" and to be generating "furious excitement" wherever it was seen. Women who wore the costume attracted huge crowds, which were generally male and often hostile. The level of public harassment was so severe that most women stopped wearing it in public after a few months, but the costume was supported by women's activists and others on the grounds that it was healthy, fostered women's independence from men by increasing their capacity for physical movement, represented independence from fashion, and fitted the values of American society—economy, utility, and comfort. However, the majority response was negative. The Bloomer costume was interpreted as a threat to the ideology of separate spheres on the grounds that it would erase all distinctions between the sexes. Victorian clothing was a form of social control which contributed to the maintenance of women in dependent, subservient roles.

According to her own account, Bloomer herself was "praised and censured, glorified and ridiculed." Owing to the amount of ridicule and censure that the costume engendered, she and her friends ceased to wear it after a few years. However, adaptations of the Bloomer costume continued to be worn in the private sphere of the home, particularly on the frontier. By the 1860s, some women had replaced the Turkish-style trousers with masculine trousers, creating costumes that prefigured the late twentieth-century pants suit. Later in the century, dress-reform patterns were available, and dress-reform styles were sold in stores.

Members of the American women's movement continued throughout the century to lobby for dress reform, forming associations, holding conventions, writing books and articles, and seeking to popularize simpler, healthier styles of dress. In 1892 and 1893, dress reformers organized a "Symposium on Dress," at which they presented three designs that included either a divided skirt or trousers. The response when members of the symposium wore these clothes on the street was much more favorable than it had been forty years before, but eventually the women ceased to wear them, too. These dress reforms were still too radical for many middle-class women and tended to alienate potential supporters of the women's rights movement, which was the principal interest of these dress reformers. . . .

The Impact of Sports on Dress

When American dress reformers wore a skirt over trousers on the street and proposed the costume for general wear, they were widely criticized, but a very similar costume, used in the same period as an exercise uniform in schools, colleges, and sanitariums, was acceptable, apparently because it was not worn on city streets. Rules governing clothing behavior in public space were characterized by subtle differences depending on location, class, and gender. For example, trousered costumes for women were permitted when swimming in the ocean but not for promenades on the beach. The introduction of new sports, particularly bicycling, during the second half of the century produced a redefinition of the way in which symbolic boundaries were expressed in public space. In a sense, alternative dress worn in public spaces was a manifestation of more radical changes that were occurring in more secluded spaces.

Until the twentieth century, sports and physical exercise as a leisure activity for women were reserved almost exclusively for the upper and upper-middle classes. What women wore while engaging in these sports depended largely upon the nature of the public spaces in which they were performed. When sports were performed near the home or in social clubs, conformity to middle-class standards of feminine dress was generally required. Tennis, croquet, ice skating, and golf were perceived as social rather than sports activities. Consequently, in the 1870s, women were expected to dress for these sports as they dressed for other social occasions: long skirts with trains, tight corsets, bustles, and large hats. When sports were played in institutions or in the countryside, sports costumes were more likely to include items of masculine clothing. Women's colleges provided settings where women could play men's sports, such as baseball, without being seen. Sports were considered a "male preserve," a means by which men proved their masculinity. Women who played men's sports in public were considered vulgar and possibly immoral.

Riding and Swimming Costumes Accepted

Riding was one of the earliest recreations in which upper-class women engaged. In the middle of the seventeenth century, the riding habit worn by women in the countryside for riding, walking, and traveling included [according to one historian] "an imitation of the wide-skirted coat then worn by men, with a similar cravat at the neck, a periwig and cocked hat on the head." Significantly, these masculine items of clothing were worn with full skirts and numerous petticoats. In the nineteenth century, women continued to wear riding habits derived from masculine clothing, but primarily for riding. Made by tailors rather than dressmakers, the sidesaddle riding habit in 1850 imitated a man's formal suit from the waist up but incorporated full and long skirts below. By the 1880s, most women wore long, straight, dark trousers underneath the skirts. They were also wearing high silk top hats, similar to those worn by men, as well as jockey caps and straw hats. By 1890, the costume from the waist up bore an even closer resemblance to male styles: "The hip-length jacket featured an open collar and lapels that revealed a hunting shirt and stock tie underneath. . . . A bowler hat or a straight hat, 'like a man's, with the addition of a veil.'" The costume still included a voluminous skirt. A new type of costume originating in London included an ankle-length frock coat over breeches. This costume was controversial because it implied that the rider rode astride rather than sidesaddle. Riding astride was not considered appropriate until after the First World War. Made in the style of men's breeches by specialized tailors, breeches were more frequently worn by women after 1900. The evolution of riding costume reveals the extent to which upper-class women wore items of masculine clothing, including various forms of trousers, which were considered totally inappropriate in other contexts.

Swimming costume was another area in which upper- and middle-class women were permitted to engage in otherwise

FASHION

inappropriate clothing behavior. Lencek and Bosker describe summer resorts as "fashion laboratories where the well-to-do came to experiment with new styles of dress and behavior." As early as the 1860s, short trousers or bloomers, which were not acceptable in other public places, were adopted for bathing

How Corsets Were Redesigned for Changing Lifestyles

By 1914 [a] popular phenomenon, the tango, [had] affected active American women's corset use. Women began removing their stiff corsets at parties in order to dance, and corset manufacturers responded once again by marketing dance corsets. But . . . corsetlessness remained a situational phenomenon practiced by a daring minority of mostly young and slim women at this time. Yet, while *Vogue* conceded in 1914 that "the mode of the corsetless figure is an established one— for a season, at least," it also noted that "the point has been reached where women do not have to be dictated to, as formerly, in the matter of corsets." Rather than doing away with corsets entirely, *Vogue* argued that since many corset models were now available "the present mode is not a uniform one. A year ago where one or two corsets would answer, it is now not a luxury, but a necessity, to have a greater number, and each of a different sort." Thus, corset manufacturers' decision to supply women with lighter and more flexible corsets was not mere concession, but also a means to increase the total number of corsets sold. Nonetheless, increasing the number of corset styles available also created a situation in which a monolithic fashionability began to dissolve, and women's power to determine their own shape within fashionability expanded.

Jill Fields, "'Fighting the Corsetless Evil': Shaping Corsets and Culture, 1900–1930," *Journal of Social History* 33 (2), pp. 355–84, 1999.

suits for women . . . and were worn with a belted jacket, for example. Byrde quotes a magazine of the period saying that young women in this costume resembled "pretty boys." In the United States, a knee-length or ankle-length skirt was worn over the trousers. Stockings were optional. By 1909, women's bathing suits had changed very little. Corsets were recommended, although the type of corset generally used was much smaller than for land wear.

Throughout this period, women were expected to wear their regular clothes—long-sleeved blouses, floor-length skirts, corsets, enormous hats, and gloves—on the beach itself, and photographs suggest that most of them did. The sea itself was defined as a liminal space in which normal sartorial (and moral) standards did not apply. The sharp segregation between land and sea was emphasized by the use of wooden huts on wheels at the water's edge, in which women changed into bathing suits and from which they entered the sea. Photographs suggest that it was not unusual for women, when wading in the ocean or in rivers fully dressed, to show bare legs, in contrast to norms that skirts should always cover the ankles. . . .

Bicycling and Women's Fashions

The impact of the bicycle on clothing behavior in the 1890s derived from its being a completely new sport and therefore not identified as a male activity. It was also an activity that was difficult to perform in privacy; it required space and public roads, although early upper-class female riders attempted to seclude themselves in public parks. The first female bicycle riders in England were society women who were driven in carriages to London parks to ride. Bicycling also differed from previous recreations in that it was virtually impossible to ride bicycles in the fashionable clothing of the period.

The most suitable costumes for bicycling were the divided skirt, which looked like a skirt but was actually a pair of very full knee-length pants, and knickerbockers. In America, the latter were widely used for about two years (1895–97) as bicycling became increasingly popular but disappeared rapidly afterward. For the most part, bloomers were worn with skirts. When women wore them without skirts, they were "jeered and scorned." The solution that was accepted by the end of the decade was shorter skirts. Women had already begun to wear shorter skirts at summer resorts in the 1890s, but the first women who wore ankle-length skirts in the city in the mid-1890s attracted hostile, shrieking crowds. In England, a few women wore bloomers; others wore a special type of skirt that could be buttoned around each leg in the form of trousers when on the machine. Outside city parks and in the country-side there was considerable resistance to the use of such costumes, particularly among the working class: [According to Rubinstein] "Women cyclists in 'rationals' met jeering crowds wherever they went and sometimes encountered violence, especially in urban areas . . . the poorer the district, the more incensed . . . the people.". . .

Pants Accepted in the United States

In the United States, between [World War I and World War II], upper- and middle-class women wore pants primarily in secluded public spaces, such as ranches and resorts. Several seemingly contradictory trends came together in the 1930s that led to trousers' being worn with greater frequency for leisure activities. Dude ranches became popular vacation spots for the middle class, and this in turn led to the introduction of dungarees for women. At the same time, Hollywood films, which were then an important influence on clothing fashions, depicted numerous strong, "masculine" heroines. Marlene Dietrich's heroines, who engaged in "cross-dressing," were probably the most powerful of these characterizations. Fisher argues that the Depression in the 1930s was a social as well as an economic crisis and produced profound anxiety about personal identity and particularly gender identity. She claims that prevailing ideas of masculinity and femininity were in flux during this period.

However, working-class women gradually assimilated trousers into their daily lives. Evidence from Sears catalogues in the 1940s and from photographs suggest that widespread acceptance of pants began among working-class women in the West, particularly California, and gradually spread to the East and the middle classes in the fifties, reversing the usual direction of fashion change, which was from east to west. Olian states: "Steadily increasing numbers of sportswear pages fea-

tured slacks. Originating in California, as befitting the informality of the West Coast lifestyle, they enjoyed great popularity for work as well as for recreation." The Second World War,
with its images of working-class women in heavy industry, reinforced this trend in its early stages. More women worked in
industry than ever before and were frequently provided with
uniforms consisting of "slacks, blouse, and visor-cap of matching material." Others wore jeans and overalls.

Feminist Objections

As they had been in the nineteenth century, feminists during
the late 1960s and the 1970s were resolutely opposed to fashionable clothing. French feminist Simone de Beauvoir performed an important role in shaping feminists' views of fashion. Unlike their predecessors, they were more critical of the
"manipulative discourses" of femininity underlying clothing
styles than of the clothes themselves. In the United States, the
first mass women's liberation movement demonstration was
directed against the Miss America beauty contest in 1968, and
specifically against the stereotype of the female body as sexual
object that the contest represented.

Again like their predecessors in the nineteenth century,
feminists in the 1970s proposed alternative modes of dress to
substitute for fashionable styles, specifically various forms of
trousers, worn with other simple and casual clothes, such as
T-shirts and low-heeled shoes. In the United States, lesbian
feminists were the most committed to rejecting any attempt
at personal adornment or body display. They wore loose-fitting
jeans or baggy workmen's denim overalls, with men's T-shirts
or work shirts and men's work boots or sneakers, and avoided
cosmetics, jewelry, or conventional haircuts. Less extreme
versions of this costume permitted fitted jeans with matching
accessories, which produced a more "becoming" look. Many
nonlesbian feminists wore dresses and long skirts or, at resorts, tight fitting pants and shirts; their appearance was very
similar to nonfeminist middle-class women. Although the
level of hostility and ridicule toward the clothing of the lesbian feminists in the early 1970s was very high, within a
decade, variations on the lesbian-feminist "style," ranging
from austere to flattering, had become the typical leisure cos-

tume of young middle-class women. The widespread acceptance of pants by middle-class women appears to have been pioneered by marginal groups within that class, specifically lesbian feminists.

The Twentieth-Century Workplace

In the late twentieth century, middle-class professional and businesswomen have not been permitted to don a totally mannish look but are still expected to retain elements of femininity in their office clothes. The short skirted business suit appeared in the 1920s and has changed relatively little in subsequent decades. In middle-class corporate workplaces, taboos against the use of trousers by women executives remain, although these women typically wear jeans and other types of trousers for leisure activities. In accordance with corporate dress codes that may or may not be explicitly defined, they are likely to wear contemporary versions of nineteenth-century alternative dress, including suit jackets and skirts, with shirts styled like men's or with silk blouses, the entire outfit in neutral, conservative colors. Now, however, these types of outfits are considered conservative rather than subversive. A fashionably feminine or seductive appearance is considered demeaning.

The contrast with working-class female employees is striking. They frequently wear uniforms that are virtually identical to those of men. In the postwar period, masculine uniforms for women gradually appeared in occupations where women were performing work similar to that of men. Englishwomen transport workers were wearing masculine uniforms in the 1940s. American police departments adopted masculine uniforms for women after Congress amended the Civil Rights Act in 1972 to prohibit state and local governments from discriminating on the basis of gender. Beginning in 1973, police departments all over the country gave women the same assignments as men, along with suitable clothing. Skirts were replaced by trousers, creating uniforms very similar to those of men, including ties, visored caps, and trousers. Subsequently, railroad conductors, nurses, and airline stewardesses, among other occupations, were assigned unisex uniforms. Similar changes have occurred in France, and the earlier restrictions on trousers for women have disappeared. Nevertheless, in the higher ranks of these occupations, one finds the same ambivalence toward the use of trousers that occurs in middle-class corporate workplaces. At work, women adapt to male cultures that vary in the extent to which women are permitted or required to "assimilate."

"Bare Limbs Will Not Be Tolerated!": Bathing Suits and Women's Rights

Angela J. Latham

One dramatic change in American fashion has been the evolution of women's bathing suits, from the nearly full-body cover-up still worn in the late 1800s to today's thong bikini. This evolution reflects not only changing tastes in clothing, but also new attitudes about health, modesty, and the female body. Bathing suits first became the focus of public controversy in the 1870s, the period when swimming became a popular national sport. Women's clothing at that time was still conservative, though feminists were beginning to rally for dress reform—more comfortable, practical clothes for everyday wear. The beach became one of the battlegrounds for the debate. "Bare limbs will not be tolerated!" warned one of the rules posted regarding women's beachwear at a 1920s Atlantic City seaside resort. Similar rules tried to regulate swimwear around the country. Many women, however, simply ignored them.

   This article discusses the bathing suit controversy of the 1920s, particularly the case of Louise Rosine, a woman who was arrested after refusing to comply with

■

the beach dress code. Rosine's case provides insights into early nineteenth century attitudes about appearance and age. Author Angela J. Latham is a scholar in theater history at Triton College in Chicago.

MANY PEOPLE PERCEIVED FASHION TRENDS OF the 1920s as nothing less than a visual synopsis of all that was morally wrong with American women. And some felt that the sartorial freedoms women began to enjoy connoted a tide of increasing moral laxity that must not merely be objected to but decisively curbed. Consequently, certain fashions for women, formerly the objects of heated debate, now were legally prohibited as well. The one-piece bathing suit, which had been popularized by the champion swimmer and later star of vaudeville and motion pictures, Annette Kellerman, was legally banned in some parts of the country. Kellerman herself was arrested for indecent exposure when she first appeared in her "body stocking" style suit at Boston's Revere Beach in 1908, and responses toward her attire would not have been much different in many places throughout the United States until late in the 1920s. Not only was the sleek Kellerman-style suit physically freeing compared with the bulky yards of fabric in which women had formerly "bathed," but it was specifically problematic in that it quite clearly revealed the contours of the female figure. The suit was doubly offensive to some when stockings were eliminated or were not worn according to regulations, which usually meant they were rolled below the knees. In any case, the "Annette Kellerman," or more simply, the one-piece bathing costume, was considered the most daring kind of bathing apparel and therefore became the focus of many censorship efforts, not to mention sarcastic innuendo.

Bathing Suit Restrictions and Public Opinion

Controversies over swimwear fashions also broadened the already gaping division among ranks of feminists. Women's reactions to bathing suit restrictions in Atlantic City in June 1921 effectively illustrate this point. The beach season opened that year with bitter sparring, publicized by the local press, over the town's bathing suit ordinances. One of the first indications that a storm was brewing was in the form of a letter written to Mayor Edward L. Bader by Mrs. John J. White in response to a recent announcement that one-piece bathing suits would be permissible in the Bathers' Revue planned for late in the summer. White accusingly asked the mayor why, when these suits had been banned, they would "now not only be permitted but invited on our Boardwalk for thousands to look at?" Mayor Bader reassured White that he appreciated her motives and had no "intention to allow anyone to parade upon the Boardwalk in any costume that may be a discredit to the Pageant Committee."

White's understanding of local ordinances was accurate, to be sure. Bathing suit regulations prohibiting one-piece suits had just recently been announced by Dr. Charles Bossert, commander of the Beach Patrol. Furthermore, all suits for women were to be "neither too low in front or back," and the attached skirts "must be of reasonable length—at least half way to the knees. Bare limbs will not be tolerated; full length hosiery must be worn." Although Mrs. White clearly wanted a strict and consistent enforcement of these rules, other Atlantic

In 1914, when these bathing beauties were photographed, many people considered their attire to be shocking and immodest.

City residents, including many young women, were incensed.

Ada Taylor, a young woman described as a Presbyterian Sunday school teacher and president of the "exclusive" Ambassador Swimming Club, wrote to Bossert, protesting the city's restrictions. She complained that "bare legged bathers attracted less attention than short-skirted, silk-stockinged wheelchair patrons" or indeed, less than "milady who rolls along the Boardwalk with legs crossed, showing her costly silk stockings at least to the knee." A more tempered letter to Mayor Bader, signed by "Miss Fenwick" and "Miss Krauth," who described themselves as "sixteen and not bold girls" but ones who were decidedly in favor of one-piece suits, argued that a "good swimmer cannot possibly swim with skirts dangling around her knees." A Newark physician, George W. Smith, also wrote to complain to Atlantic City's mayor. His letter, printed in the local newspaper, indicates—and quite possibly exaggerates—the magnitude of the city's quarrel. "Dear Sir—Thousands of people are getting disgusted with Atlantic City as far as beach regulations are concerned. The people who wear short bathing suits, allowing the feet and lower limbs to have the benefit of the water are all right. Anybody knows that the action of the water is more beneficial without stockings than with them." In spite of pragmatic appeals like this one, many people still felt that morality, not better swimming, was the crux of this controversy. The Atlantic City Rotary Club even staged a debate on the question of whether or not one-piece costumes were "conducive to morality.". . .

No Standard Dress Codes

Although debates as to what constituted proper bathing attire certainly occurred between women, this was by no means an issue left to women to decide for themselves. Not only resort towns like Atlantic City but most cities that had public bathing facilities or beaches had regulations by which to govern bathers' appearance. As with proscriptions against short skirts, however, in the early 1920s local municipalities throughout the United States varied considerably in terms of interest in and approaches to the regulation of bathing costumes. Some communities had quite heavy-handed means of enforcing bathing dress codes, while others seemed virtually unconcerned about female swim attire. These differences are difficult to account for consistently or explain rationally. For example, while it was generally true that resort areas in Florida and California were among the least restrictive in the regulation of bathing costumes, it is not possible to conclude from this that coastal regions were more lenient than inland areas. Throughout the East Coast there were heated debates over women's swimwear, with significant differences in dress codes for bathing from one town to another. And while bathers in some California and Florida cities may have been relatively at their ease in what they chose to wear on the beach, it is no doubt true that the restrictiveness of codes varied in these states as well.

Chicago was comparatively censorious about women's swimwear. . . . Within the first few days after the opening of the beach season in June 1921, Chicago's deputy commissioner of public works, William Burkhardt, announced that bathing costumes would no longer be left to the consciences of the women who wore them, as had been the case the previous summer. Burkhardt felt it necessary to impose more precise regulations for the new season since, referring to last year's bathers, "[s]ome of them apparently didn't have any such thing as a conscience." For emphasis, he added, "If it had not been for the unsympathizing policewomen on duty the city's beaches would have looked like a second garden of Eden. No, sir, we are not leaving anything to conscience this year. . . .

The Arrest of Louise Rosine

The sometimes extreme opposition between forces for and against the rights of a woman to define "suitable" bathing attire for herself are nowhere more vividly illustrated than in an incident leading to the arrest of Louise Rosine, a resident of Los Angeles who visited Atlantic City in the late summer of 1921. Rosine's rejection of what she felt were unreasonable dress codes and the circumstances surrounding her blatant defiance of them provide a vivid glimpse of the clash between opposing ideologies of "appropriate" femininity that coexisted in American culture in the early 1920s.

Rosine's ordeal began when she refused to roll up her stockings to cover her knees when ordered to do so by a police officer. News reports of the incident describe this recalcitrant woman in detail, compared with many women noted in stories about noncompliance with bathing suit regulations throughout the early 1920s. Readers learned not only her name and where she was from, but also that Rosine was a novelist, thirty-nine years of age. Several accounts of her arrest, at least four of which were in New York newspapers, quoted and paraphrased her opinions at length. While such attention to her views may seem an attempt to represent her side of the story fairly, the feeling one gets when reading any of the reports of Rosine's arrest and eventual imprisonment is that of being audience to a freak show. If accurately reported, Rosine's actions were indeed unorthodox, yet her reduced status as outsider or "other" was clearly stressed by journalists. Furthermore, her arresting officer and even the warden of the prison where she was detained were portrayed as abused victims of her unruly behavior, in spite of their clearly marked status as empowered authorities in the situation.

Except for minor variations, the following report is representative of those published by New York newspapers.

> Miss Louise Rosine . . . most emphatically declared to-day it was "none of the city's business whether she 'rolled her stockings up or down,'" and is now in the City Jail in a state of mutiny and uncovered knees. She has avowed she will fight her arrest in the courts, even if it must go to the United States Supreme Court.

> Miss Rosine appeared on the Virginia Avenue beach this morning with her stockings rolled below her knees. Beach Policeman Edward Shaw informed her courteously that it was against the regulations here.

> "I most certainly will not roll 'em up," she retorted. "The city has no right to tell me how I shall wear my stockings. It is none of its business. I will go to jail first."

> The policeman then said he would have to take her there. As he took her by the arm she is alleged to have swung a right to the officer's eye, nearly flooring him. He recovered and blew his whistle. Life guards responded and Miss Rosine was taken to the jail in the wagon.

The officer, his glasses broken and his dignity ruffled, has preferred a charge of assault and battery in addition to disorderly conduct against Miss Rosine.

Advised by the police matron to roll up her stockings, the novelist still refused, and, according to the latest reports, is occupying a cell in the glory of uncovered knees. She has, further, refused to try to get bail.

Inappropriate Remarks

In contrast to New York news coverage which, as shown here, focused on the violent encounter between Rosine and Officer Edward Shaw, the *Atlantic City Daily Press* report about the incident emphasized events following her incarceration in the city's jail, as well as even more personal and, by today's standards, inappropriate commentary about Rosine herself.

Beneath the title of the local report on the arrest, a subheading proclaimed: "Arrested for Clawing Beachcop When She Refused to 'Roll 'Em Up,' Pacific Coast Visitor Takes Off Bathing Suit in Cell and 'September Morns.'" Obviously poking fun, the reporter next announced that Rosine weighed over two hundred pounds. Not content to leave this point alone, however, the reporter also stated that Rosine weighed "as much as [boxer] Jack Dempsey and looks as powerful." This intentionally unflattering portrayal was repeated again in the lengthy account when, in describing her scuffle with Officer Shaw, the author noted:

First was a righthand wallop that landed with Dempseyan precision on Shaw's nose. Then Miss Rosine crossed with her left a bit higher, smashing the policeman's glasses and ruining his coat of tan with painful lacerations. They clinched.

No referee volunteered to break them and Miss Rosine, using her weight, Shaw estimated it at "210 or more," gave a snappy exhibition of in-fighting, sadly mussing up the policeman's features. Exhausted from the rain of blows, she freed Shaw, who charges she then fastened her teeth in hi[s] wrist.

. . . A cursory examination of women's fashion in the 1920s reveals that a youthful and slim appearance was considered ideal.

The fashion industry itself was quite unambiguous as to which women looked best in the newest styles, and it communicated this information largely through the women it selected as models. But there were clearly many other means by which permission was granted or denied to women who wished to dress fashionably. Reformers commonly belittled some women in the apparent attempt to shame them into dressing "appropriately."

Certainly, Rosine was perceived to be obese, but undoubtedly she was also considered too old to be dressed as she was according to standards of beauty that had by this time come into vogue. Age was clearly a factor in these bathing costume controversies, not only in terms of differing feminist philosophies but also in terms of aesthetics and propriety. One Kentucky senator, for example, speaking in support of a bill he had proposed to regulate women's swimwear and thus "protect the eyes of the old men and the morals of the young men, claimed that it was "an awfully pitiful sight to see an old, gray-haired woman with her skirts above her knees." Rosine's "unacceptable" body presence, coupled with her willingness to expose that presence, was itself an act of nonconformity. Although an attractive, unmarried flapper of twenty might sun herself on the sands of a resort area without drawing suspicion, an overweight, thirty-nine-year-old single woman who proclaimed herself a novelist and vacationed far from home, apparently without a companion, was surely trying to create a stir. After all, even flappers, at some point in their youth, were expected to settle down as devoted wives and mothers. In these ways, Rosine not only defied the beach codes of Atlantic City but much more pervasive cultural expectations about femininity as well.

The Psychology of Victoria's Secret

Nancy V. Workman

Victoria's Secret is one of the most popular women's
lingerie brands in the United States. The clothing
line is sold in boutiquelike shops throughout the
country and via mail-order catalogs. Business experts
agree that part of the success of the line is due to Victoria's Secret's marketing strategy. The stores are designed to recreate a nineteenth-century bedroom, literally transporting customers into the Victorian age.

In this essay, Nancy V. Workman examines what she
calls the "social psychology" of the Victoria's Secret
stores and merchandise. She discusses the corset—the
Victorian women's undergarment that was worn tightly
around the waist. Workman explains how this earlier
fashion trend may have been a way to control women
and their sexuality. She argues that while Victoria's Secret does not sell corsets, their marketing campaign
uses and promotes similar nineteenth-century ideas
about women's bodies and femininity. Workman is a
member of the department of English at Lewis University in Romeoville, Illinois.

IN 1986, VICTORIA'S SECRET, THE SPECIALTY LIN-
gerie store that is owned in America by The Limited, was a
franchise of 167 stores with an annual sales volume of 112 million dollars. However, by 1990, those numbers rose dramatically; the mail order catalogue sales alone totalled over $250
million dollars worth of fashion and accessories. Even in a re-

■

cession marked by the failure of many merchandising retailers and generally sluggish sales of clothing, Sue Woodman points out that Victoria's Secret was a notable exception. In fact, according to a *Business Week* article, Victoria's Secret "now sells more lingerie under that label in its 353 stores than industry stalwarts Vanity Fair and Maidenform."

In most cases, the franchise offers a diverse product line which includes underwear and sleepwear, as well as seasonal wear, from many eras. As the catalogues indicate, however, the store specializes in lingerie, displayed and marketed against backgrounds that are suggestively English and nineteenth century. The original store design was deliberately that of a "'turn-of-the-century San Francisco bordello,'" but the design has been modified to be "lighter and airier, 'more like a bedroom setting, very personalized.'" The store fixtures suggest bedroom ambience and are chosen to evoke a personal intimacy, not a sales display area. Thus, merchandise is stored in pull-out drawers that resemble bedroom furniture, and contemporary bras are displayed in ornate frames suggestive of Rossetti's Jane Morris paintings but disguised to look like the actual possessions of "Victoria," the store owner.

The Victorian theme in the showroom periodically changes to reflect new merchandising strategies, but it always retains the Victorian connection. For example, during the 1991 season, small showcases depicting a line of books, entitled *Words of Victoria*, lined the shelves. More recently, small Victorian baby carriages, complete with porcelain faced dolls of the era, stand alongside the lingerie displays. In addition to the showroom, the merchandise also bears a Victorian and English connection. For example, in the "Summer Sale '91" catalogue, sleepwear is advertised as "decorated with a traditional English yellow and rose print" with suitable names such as "Westbury pyjama," or "Canterbury Nightdresses," or yet again, "The Somerset Boxer Pyjama Set." The respective names evoke geographic connections to England, a deliberate association on the part of the merchandiser.

Regardless of the diversity of the clothing line, however, the Victoria's Secret franchises sell a line of underwear patterned after garments such as the corset and bodysuit that had been popular in Queen Victoria's day. Replacing the whalebone stays and rigid structures of the originals with more natural fibers and materials such as lycra and spandex, these corsets nonetheless continue the association of Victorian sexuality, coupling eroticism with the illicit and forbidden. This article examines the "social psychology" of Victoria's Secret, especially its use of the Victorian corset, by showing the connection between contemporary culture and the high culture of Victorian fashion. It will uncover some of the cultural meanings that are associated with foundation garments, comparing the Victorian "meanings" with more modern ones.

History of the Corset

Many early fashion historians have traced the history of the corset as part of women's apparel by seeing connections between the shapes of women's bodies and more comprehensive trends in art and design. Thus, they rarely see history of the corset in isolation. Rather, they see it against the backdrop of cultural trends. For example, in *A History of Ladies Underwear*, Cecil Saint-Laurent suggests that the revival of the corset in the nineteenth century was part of a general movement of shapes: "From 1775 to 1800, shapes, whether in architecture, furniture or clothes, had tended to lose their roundness and had become elongated, straight and light; . . . between 1820 and 1850 they returned to cambers and curves, with narrowness as a contrast." The corset, with its ability to tightly emphasize a woman's form, pushed up the breasts while simultaneously outlining the hips, giving women an overall appearance of ample curves, albeit a distorted one: "Still bound and sealed up, more crippled and crushed than ever, women in 1900 just looked strange. From their appearance, it seemed as though they had no spinal column or abdomen, only an enormous behind; in short, they looked less human than women did in the farthingale." . . .

While critics disagree on the exact number of women who used corsets on a daily basis during the nineteenth century, nonetheless, they agree that the corset "enormously exaggerated" the "minimal differences between the physical anatomy of men and women" and that the corset was symbolic of the roles which women were forced to play during that era. Greatly restricted by social conventions, women's roles were confining and painful, and the corset epitomized women's plight as "exquisite slave." According to Helene Roberts, women "had been taught that submissiveness and pain were related, and that they were women's lot." Starting as young girls, women were conditioned to "cage" their bodies by using painful lacings to reduce the size of their waist. Studying women's magazines and memoirs, Roberts traces a typical lacing history as the young girl progressed from "baby stays" to an "unboned, tight fitting corset" and finally the severely compressed version so tight that it required the assistance of a maid or other woman to pull its strictures.

Negative Physical and Emotional Aspects

The physical consequences of wearing the corset were enormous. In addition to weakening muscles by preventing them from becoming developed, the corset caused actual illness by restricting the normal flow of air to the lungs and diaphragm, sometimes even causing death. Whether fatal or not, the corset also caused women to feel a "general weakness," a "sense of languor and fatigue" because of the ways in which it prevented movement and exercise. In addition, wearing the corset became a necessity, even at night, as the bindings were only loosened for a few inches for fear that a women's waist would expand too much if left uncorsetted over a long period of time. Furthermore, the corset was related to the class system as corsets were traditionally worn by middle-class and upper-class women who did not need to perform manual labor. Like other aspects of Victorian culture, the corset materially separated women from one another.

In addition to the physical demands of corset wearing, Roberts shows the ways in which corsets were coupled with Victorian morality and standards. For example, she insists that wearing the corset became "a moral imperative" since uncorsetted women were seen to be loose or immoral. Thus, tight lacing was seen as "moral rectitude" by which a woman exercised control over her natural body, restricting it and covering her nakedness. However, the clothing symbolism was highly charged. On the one hand, the corsetted woman was modest since she covered all her body with both underwear and clothing, rarely exposing cleavage as had been the norm in earlier eras. On the other hand, the corset drew attention to those bodily aspects of breasts and hips that the clothing covered by distorting them in size and shape. Not surprisingly, what resulted was a fetishism, an abnormal attention to women's body shapes. More importantly, the corset became an eroticized article of underclothing.

The Creation of Victoria's Secret

It is difficult to analyze the recent revival of the corset as an article of contemporary erotica. Nonetheless, in this section, I wish to examine some of the cultural implications of the Victorian revival. I shall show how the commercial forces which dictate gendered clothing not only distort the historical period in question, but bring to the modern consciousness racist and classist notions of the female body, ones that render modern women psychologically inferior, indeed as "mad."

In addition to reinforcing traditional sex roles, the revival of the Victorian corset as an article of erotic wear is a manufactured revival, carefully controlled by merchandisers and ad agents. . . .

The "look" of Victoria's Secret shops is an adman's fantasy, not the collective effort of a subgroup of contemporary women. In America, the look is created and governed by James Mansour, who serves as the director of design and research for The Limited. Using the New York Madison Avenue store as a "laboratory," Mansour tests new ideas and products before creating less expensive copies for the other national outlets. Thus, in the New York store, $15,000 tables sit beside $10,000 clocks; mannequins from England, whose complexion is "pink and pearlized," are sprayed each morning with a scent to create a particular atmosphere in the store. According to Mansour, this "adds to the subliminal impact." Later, these same touches will be duplicated so that shoppers in malls across the country experience the Victorian ambience of the outlets. So controlled is the "look" that analysts conclude Mansour "is actively involved in new prototype design. From hangers and fixtures to music and advertising, nothing escapes his attention." His approach is a conscious and aggressive manipulation of desire.

Thus, the commercialization of Victoriana is a major factor in its cultural significance. The enormous profits which are realized by the original franchises have not gone unnoticed by discount merchandisers who have started to manufacture and sell less expensive lingerie using the "Victoria's Secret" look. According to an unnamed buyer for a New England chain, "It's a Victoria's Secret look. Basically, that's what I look for in my department, to bring in looks that are popular and successful in Victoria's Secret but at my price points." From this trend, it is obvious that commercial forces continue to replace the social and moral ones in determining what is appropriate wear for contemporary women. As well as being victims of a moral order that insists the body be confined to be desirable, women are increasingly victimized by a culture which saturates the marketplace with items that are manufactured needs. As Kunzle concludes, "The once-repressed sexualization of dress is now the object of massive and relentless commercialization. It is not the sexualization of the past, but it's commercialization in the present, which is the obstacle to progress."

Reinforcing the Message

These commercial forces which bind women psychologically are reinforced in other aspects of the Victorian revival which marks Victoria's Secret. For example, the selections of books which were sold in 1995, the *Words of Victoria* series, are clearly manipulated to reflect a certain notion of female behavior. In the introduction to the first volume, *Words of Love*, the imaginary Victoria justifies the pictorial selections accompanying the text in the volume by saying, "My choice has inevitably included paintings by those unashamedly romantic Victorian artists, for there can be nothing more lovely than their descriptions of wistful women in flowing robes, detailed in satin or lace, or more dashing than their portrayal of the young gentlemen of Victorian England." Thus, John Everett Millais's "Black Brunswicker" illustrates a text called, "You are a Prisoner, Miss," a selection actually taken from Thomas Hardy's *Far from the Madding Crowd*, the scene in which Bathsheba attempts to pull away from the embraces of the "dashing soldier."

Lest the notion of sexual capture, whether by a man or a woman, be lost on the reader, the Preface to volume four, the *Beauty of Love*, informs them that women's charms and beauty have held "poets and painters in thrall throughout history" and that "all have the power to enslave." Including excerpts from George Eliot, Tennyson, Hardy and Gaskell, the book is designed to reinforce the "mystery" of female beauty which is not only a "charm" but a "peril" to men throughout the world. Women's beauty can "strike awe in the heart of the beholder." Again, the text echoes the nineteenth century debates regarding women's roles, the debates which insisted on the limitations of women's sexuality for fear that it would prove too difficult for men to address. Furthermore, the store name underscores the same message—a secret can be charming and mysterious, but it can also be sinister and deadly.

Use of Stereotypes

These explicit "historical traces" of Victoriana not only romanticize Victorian culture, but blatantly reinforce sexist and demeaning pictures of sexual interaction. Purposely ignoring all the undercurrents of Victorian literature which repeatedly stressed the inherent limitations of sexual relationships in the nineteenth century, these books celebrate the nostalgic, the flowery Valentine tradition of Victorian sentimentality and melodrama. Not surprisingly, then, another product line sold in Victoria's Secret is stationery, particularly blank sheets bordered by smiling cherubs and flowery overabundance.

As a result, the shopper is saturated on every level with sensory cues which connect what can only be seen as the most maudlin aspects of Victorian culture. And the saturation exists on the literal level—the volumes of *Victoria's Words* are perfumed, wrapped in cellophane so that opening them releases a powerful sweet smelling odor, one associated with the bathing products also sold on the premises. In visual as well as non-visual ways the shopper is assaulted with cultural messages from every art form. Today, gender "corsetting" is determined by the "stays" of mixed media.

This cultural saturation is a distortion of authentic Victorian culture, whether British or American. Furthermore, the sexual undercurrents so stressed within the Victoria's Secret stores create a sexual claustrophobia for it is impossible to escape the deliberate ways in which fashion is being dictated in every square foot of sales space. In addition, the fact that underwear is now also outerwear, as evidenced by Madonna in her public appearances, suggests the total identification of the erotic with what had formerly been clothing worn for very different reasons. Nonetheless, the notion still prevails that nakedness is not erotic and that women's bodies need to be shaped to be seen as desirable.

Undergarments and Femininity

To explain this emphasis of underwear as erotic, Subrata N. Chakravarty places Victoria's Secret within an historical context. In doing so, she unconsciously shows the extent to which women are being savagely manipulated. For example, she notes that during the emancipated sixties, many women left off wearing bras and corsets because they were associated with a "sexist society." Seen as "restrictive, cumbersome, drab, overly structured," they were abandoned as a political protest. However, as the lingerie "industry languished," merchandisers responded by presenting these undergarments as "accessories," rather than as necessities, which they had been in earlier eras. By introducing new fabrics, colors and designs, the manufacturers were able to revitalize a sagging industry.

However, in doing so, they deliberately reinscribed the notion that women should not challenge the status quo too much. Addressing the women who had chosen to remove their bras, the fashion designers reminded them that womanliness meant "sexiness," not intellectual competence or professional achievement, even in the workplace. Chakravarty summarizes, "Many females agreed to buy such products both as a reaction to the very conservative clothing they felt to be impelled to wear on the job and as a personal reassurance against the resentment of male colleagues who have questioned the femininity of female competition in the workplace." Woodman concurs; she speaks of the success of Victoria's Secret in terms of its emphasis on "unabashed femininity."

Thus, to remain feminine, it was necessary for women to privately wear undergarments which associated them with the old traditional divisions between the sexes. Instead of redefining feminine in the light of new socio-economic conditions, women were told to regress, to return to antiquated notions of female desirability and role. Chakravarty labels this phenomenon, "The Cleopatra Syndrome." Quoting an investment banker who has made millions of dollars off of this trend, Chakravarty says that women who must "prove themselves" during the day, are now told to "gratify" themselves at night. Hence, ads emphasize "feeling good," "feel[ing] beautiful, sensuous, and desirable." Reinscribing the sexual stereotype, the ads imply that women reveal their true natures AFTER work; that a woman cannot be thought feminine while competent or business-like. . . .

Thus, the revitalization of the Victorian corset as a form of contemporary erotica is not an innocent merchandising trend. In addition to being dominated by commercial forces which ensnare women, this trend distorts the Victorian era by decontextualizing its artifacts, while nonetheless carrying forward into the modern era notions of female inferiority. Just as the Victorian corset united notions of respectable morality and sexuality, the modern corset defines women's bodies as sexually desirable, yet encloses women in rigid positions of cultural enslavement.

The Impossible Ideal: How Barbie Creates Poor and Unrealistic Body Image in Girls

Ingeborg Majer O'Sickey

Barbie dolls are synonymous with American girls' fashion. One of the most popular toys ever invented, Barbie has provided American preteen girls with inspiration of how to look and dress for decades. The doll's manufacturer, Mattel, has created spin-off characters, doll clothing, books, board games, computer software, and other Barbie-related items. Many of the Barbie products emphasize fashion and the fashion industry. The dolls continue to be best-sellers into the twenty-first century; however, not everyone thinks Barbie is a positive influence. Critics say that Barbie's appearance is an unrealistic role model for girls. Barbie's exaggerated physical dimensions—36-18-33 if she were a real woman—are literally impossible to achieve.

This article discusses the effect of Barbie on girls' perceptions of their bodies. Specifically, the essay focuses on *Barbie Magazine*, a bimonthly magazine for preteen Barbie fans that the author compares to adult fashion magazines such as *Vogue* in its style and content.

■

Author Ingeborg Majer O'Sickey argues that stories and advertisements in the magazine reinforce female stereotypes—the idea that there is one correct "look" for women—and that the magazine trains young girls to be fashion consumers. Ingeborg Majer O'Sickey is assistant professor of German at SUNY/Binghamton.

BARBIE IS INDISPUTABLY THE MOST SUCCESSFUL doll ever marketed. One sign of its success is that it has "broken out of Toyland and moved into Artville," as Alice Kahn puts it in her article "A Onetime Bimbo Becomes a Muse." Barbie populates the avenues of Artville in a variety of guises: Marge Piercy wrote a poem about her, performance artist Jeffrey Essmann impersonated her, Andy Warhol painted her, designers like Oscar de la Renta and Bob Mackie fashioned gowns for her, Kenneth and Vidal Sassoon coiffed her, New York's Modern Museum of Art, London's Victoria and Albert Museum, Washington's Smithsonian Institution, and the Oakland Museum exhibited her.

Perhaps the most impressive testimony to the doll's power came in 1986 when Mattel financed a $1.5 million exhibition titled "The Barbie Retrospective and New Theater of Fashion." The multimedia show, which was organized by BillyBoy, "a self-confessed Barbie maniac," toured Europe with a production that would rival that of any mega rock star: top couturiers from both sides of the Atlantic designed sixty original outfits, and artists created life-size Barbie habitats and holograms in celebration of Barbie's consumer euphoria. After its European tour the show climaxed in a New York extravaganza during which Warhol unveiled his painting of Barbie and 1,300 guests danced until dawn to "Barbie and the Rockers."

Clearly, Barbie had moved beyond her original doll-dom and gone . . . on to become an icon on America's Main Street. From the moment she made her grand entrance at the New York Toy Fair in 1959, Barbie Doll became the consummate material toy-girl, a role model for many members of the Baby Boomer generation. As a late-twentieth-century icon Barbie's success is measurable in hard currency: conceived as the most acquisitive doll in history, Barbie, the brainchild of Mattel Toy

Company founders Ruth and Elliot Handler, earned over $700 million in 1990 alone. *In toto*, Barbie and her entourage of family, friends, and pets have inspired a labor-intensive industry that has produced 600 million plastic dolls and more than one billion outfits, including 1.2 million pair of shoes and 35,000 handbags.

BarbieMania inspires collectors to travel from all corners of the world to Barbie conventions. Over 500 Barbie-collecting aficionados attended a three-day-long "Barbie Forever Young Convention" in Garden Grove, California. They came to buy, sell, and trade Barbie items, from plastic bags containing Skipper shoes for $1.00 to a $1,000 Barbie Airplane. BarbieMania has motivated one woman to set up the Barbie Hall of Fame in Palo Alto, California; it boasts more than 16,000 dolls in a permanent exhibit. Barbiephiliacs have been regaled with a number of Barbie biographies during the last decade, from Susan and Paris Manos's *The World of Barbie Dolls: An Illustrated Value Guide* to BillyBoy's *Barbie: Her Life and Times*.

The fashion industry has capitalized on BarbieMania as well. Mattel's designers copy Parisian haute couture for Barbie, who "possesses a specially-designed outfit for every occasion that could possibly enter a little girl's dreams." Cultural mimic and culturally mimicked, Barbie has inspired, as *Elle* documents in a photo-fashion spread titled "What a Doll!," a number of top designers to "toy with the look of America's favorite doll, in sixties suits made modern." . . .

Barbie Magazine

In 1965 more than 100,000 readers subscribed to the bimonthly magazine for girls aged four to twelve. The current textual wing of the Barbie doll, *Barbie Magazine*, was started in winter 1984. . . . At first glance, the magazine seems merely another money-making dimension of the Barbie doll. Undeniably, the magazine makes no secret of its function as a showcase to sell more in-house Mattel products. But it is not that simple. *Barbie Magazine*'s primary function is the production and reproduction of images of certain kinds of femininity in order to train girls to become perfect consumers of beautifying commodities. All women's fashion and beauty magazines are ultimately manuals for particular kinds of training in femininity; *Barbie Magazine* is the preparatory text, the basic-training manual, for the girls' later reading of teen magazines like *Seventeen* and *Mademoiselle*. These, in turn, prime teens for adult fashion magazines like *Glamour, Elle*, and *Vogue*.

The role of *Barbie Magazine* within the larger context of adult women's fashion and beauty magazines cannot be over-emphasized. Whereas these magazines are a part of the vast American apparatus of industries that sell feminizing products, *Barbie Magazine* works for these industries by laying the textual groundwork for what the plastic doll personifies: the girls are not only instructed in consumerism, but taught to accept their passage from childhood to adolescence in terms of commodities. *Barbie Magazine* builds upon ideas the doll manifests, and it initiates its readers into practices that adult women's magazines will continue. Essential to the magazine's lessons on femininity is the premise that being feminine is to be in constant need of "aesthetic innovation"; to teach girls that women, like cars, must be restyled every year. . . .

The Fashion Layouts

Editorial fashion layouts segment the children's time into slots of specific activities. Specialized "theme" clothing, such as clothes for school, sports events, parties, and holidays, suggest that the accoutrements are more important than the activities. In one such layout, titled "Jungle Fever," the models are photographed in "safari attire" against a background of junglelike vegetation. The implicit suggestion is that they need new outfits in order to have an "adventurous" play time. The theme approach to fashion camouflages this suggestion, however, in that it pretends to educate the children about cultures other than their own. But as is evident from the copy that accompanies the photographs of the little girls "in" the jungle, this "other" world is completely stripped of otherness and denuded of difference: "If you are heading south to explore the Amazon, or whether you're just taking a few fashion cues out of Africa, the jungle look is hot stuff this spring! So let *Barbie Magazine*'s models guide you on a style safari." The text's allusion to the film *Out of Africa* and its pop descriptions of Africa homogenize this other world into a commodity for the children's consumption.

Another conspicuous example of presenting children's clothes in terms of theme clothing is the fashion layout "Flamenco Fashion." Here the models (ranging in age from six to ten) are posed in what is popularly conceived to be Spanish ethnic clothing. The copy makes believe that the feature will teach children something about Spanish culture: "If you have a passion for fashion, you'll fall for these fabulous fall styles. They have a romantic tale to tell and they tell it in an exotic Spanish accent! Flamenco fashion is a fiery look that will remind you of fearless toreadors, singing troubadours, and lovely ladies with red roses."

As is clear from the trivialized and highly romanticized descriptions of other cultures, however, the world presented in these fashion editorials is a world that is finally not outside at all. It is imploded into the compass of the department-store-like world created by the Barbie doll and the magazine and then consumed by the magazine's child-reader. The self-contained consumers' world that we find in the magazine's editorials fosters a fantasy of power in the readers that ultimately backfires. The fashion spreads encourage the little girls to strive to achieve a role, but since roles based upon merchandise require no investment of the self on the part of the little girl, they are empty and, therefore, ultimately deeply frustrating.

Pressure to Be Women

A similar fantasy of power is promoted in advertisements in *Barbie Magazine.* An especially striking example is a full-page ad for the girls' streetwear line called "Unique." The child model is posed sitting on a railing with sailboats in the background. She is dressed in a feminized sailor outfit, with a seductively unbuttoned white shirt; the upturned collar and loosened tie create a look of throwaway chic. The slogan "She's unique!" is printed in a slanted position toward the focal point of the photo (the girl's head), in the top left corner of the photograph. The girl is set in affluent surroundings, whose status is condensed (and collapsed) into a code, the Yachting Club. Set against this background, the image of the little girl in "unique" clothing suggests to its readers that the identity of a female person is to be on display as affluent, white, blonde, blue-eyed, and slim. That she is said to be unique at the same time as she is used to seduce many others to become like her seems at first a contradiction. The claim is justified, however, since her image can command her spectators' gaze without returning it. Her image "receives" its viewers' envious looks only as a recognition of its own supposed self-sufficiency. The model's self-absorbed look reflects the Freudian view of the female as passive and ultimately narcissistic.

This view of women has been reproduced in countless representations of women from paintings to advertisement. Only the most self-confident among the young viewers of the photographed girl can avoid feeling somehow lacking, somehow insufficient by comparison with the self-regarding girl in the photograph. The only way the girls can escape the anxiety of insufficiency is by identifying with the photographed girl in order to compete with her. The two emotional axes activated by the advertisement, then, are identification and competition. These axes make it impossible for the girls to accept or appreciate their own difference and thus block feelings of self-worth. In that the advertisement constructs in its targeted viewers a self that is chronically insufficient, it stifles the possibility for meaningful, noncompetitive interaction with others. That this model is said to be "unique" *like* the name of the line of clothes she is advertising is another example of an explicit collapse of girl into product.

Barbie Represents the Ideal

The degree to which the idea that women are the product and the product is the woman has become introjected in mainstream American thought becomes especially clear in *Barbie 30th Anniversary Magazine*, in which Barbie's career from 1959 to 1989 is documented. A central feature in this special issue, a five-page spread entitled "Here's to You! A Celebrity Tribute to Barbie," promotes the illusion that the 11½-inch plastic doll is a human celebrity. Even though the comments celebrating Barbie's thirtieth birthday are made by prominent people of varying ages and professions, their testimonials are remarkably similar. What is significant is that their remarks about the doll's conspicuous consumption, resistance to water-weight gain, cellulite-free body, and the fact that it doesn't have to go on diets and won't get crow's feet or need a "tummy tuck" are made in an anxious humor that reflects the four major cultural anxieties in the United States: affluence, age, weight, and feminine beauty.

The celebrities cited in *Barbie 30th Anniversary Magazine* relate these anxieties misogynistically by contrasting Barbie's appearance to their own. Danielle Steel's remarks are representative of the edge to some of the observations:

> Most of us face 30 with trauma, trepidation, and terror, I approached my 30th birthday as though it were an impending earthquake. . . . Only later did I realize that women are at their most beautiful at 30. So it is with Barbie, who has turned 30 with luxuriant hair, a tiny waist, firm arms, slim thighs and a huge wardrobe.

Whereas we hear an unmistakable tone of anxiety and competition in the women's testimonials, the men's reveal the confidence of those who consider themselves to be authorities on female beauty. Designer Bill Blass puts it epigrammatically: "Happy Anniversary—you've never looked better!" Beauty Queen crowner Bert Parks gushes: "Having crowned 25 Miss Americas, I am somewhat of an authority on beauty, and Barbie, you are among the prettiest. You are the personification of eternal youth, and you have inspired many generations of young girls." Oscar de la Renta remarks, "Barbie is the ideal customer. She looks like a perfect size 6, and she keeps her figure. She's the all-American girl," unwittingly revealing the correlation between Barbie, the commodity, and women, the consumer.

Of course, Mattel's public relation move to make Barbie one of the celebrities for girls to emulate reflects a fact already "understood" by its consumers. Judging from the letters to the magazine, the girls who play with Barbie play-act as if she were a unique, grown-up star, and often in scenarios in which they "become" dolls, or, perhaps more to the point, "miniature women." One reader writes, "Dear Barbie, what I like best about your magazine are the hairstyles. I wear them all the time and I get ideas for Barbie's hairstyles, too." Another girl writes: "Dear BARBIE Magazine, one day I was thinking about what to wear. Then I opened BARBIE Magazine and found a *great* idea!" *Barbie Magazine*'s boast that "all little girls could see themselves in Barbie's eyes" is taken more than literally by its readers. Indeed, the way the magazine fulfills its dual function of promoting Mattel products and encouraging acceptance of a particular feminine beauty ideal in its readers makes clear that play with a Barbie doll is pre-scripted in a way that circumscribes the girls' play in the narrowest sense.

Growing Up Fast with Britney Spears: Celebrity Influences on Girls' Clothing

Nadya Labi

Rock stars often inspire American fashion, especially adolescent styles. One recent example is the belly-bearing trend fueled by pop idol Britney Spears. Britney's scantily clad performances have impacted the way teen girls dress—and think about their own bodies. Many critics feel that Spears's influence on fashion has left girls feeling compelled to dress in sexy clothes to gain approval from their peers, especially boys. The trend toward increasingly erotic dress has prompted some schools to enact dress codes forbidding clothes that are deemed too revealing. Schools charge that such outfits are distracting and trigger "bad attitudes."

The following article, which originally appeared in *Time* magazine, discusses how Britney Spears has influenced several teens—and preteens—around the country. The author also explores how the growing popularity of sexy adolescent clothing is resulting in related consumer goods including cosmetics and teen salons. Author Nadya Labi is a *Time* staff writer.

■

RACHEL MARTIN'S PRESENT FOR HER NINTH birthday came wrapped in silver spandex. The 5-ft. 7-in. gift walked in on a red carpet, stripped off her floor-length black coat to reveal silver hip huggers and a matching tube top and sang, "I think I did it again/I made you believe. . . ." And for a few wondrous moments, Rachel and her 10 girlfriends did believe that Britney Spears was in the house, lip-synching in front of the marble fireplace and rocking chair in Rachel's North Salem, N.Y., living room. On this recent Saturday, Shannon Connor, 21, an impersonator in hot demand at birthday parties throughout the New York City area, chose one of her more modest costumes, opting against what she refers to as the "nude outfit." She explains, "I think it would be too much for the families."

Indeed, it was just such a getup—the infamously skimpy outfit Britney wore at last September's MTV Video Music Awards—that confirmed the star's transformation from perky ingenue to pop tart. In 1999, Britney was a former Mouseketeer with a No. 1 album, . . . *Baby, One More Time*. By the time she released her second album last spring, *Oops! . . . I Did It Again*, she had grown up, gaining breasts (by what means remains unclear) and losing all inhibition. . . . And while continuing to promote her wholesome attitudes, she is enticing a legion of young fans into a world that is anything but G-rated.

Britney's impact is everywhere—in the tube tops, hip huggers and glitter makeup that girls ranging from just past toddler to barely into their teens are snapping up at stores like the Limited Too and GapKids. Girls who only a moment ago played with Barbie now play at being Britney. "Walk around any shopping mall, and you'll see mirror images of her all over the place," says Larry Flick, an editor at the music trade magazine *Billboard*. Some schools are cracking down on the lookalikes, stiffening dress codes to stamp out racy attire. Parents, for their part, are rolling their eyes and trying to walk the line between fashion and fascism.

"I like wearing shorts and skirts that show my stomach," says Tonya Rodriguez, an eighth-grader at Seven Springs Middle School in New Port Richey, Fla. "I have a really flat stomach, and I like it." Her principal, Roni Sushko, isn't quite so charmed. She has cited Tonya, 13, for dress-code violations eight times since the beginning of the school year, suspending her on two of those occasions. Tonya's infractions include wearing miniskirts and spaghetti-strap tops, which run afoul of regulations that the school's county instituted last year. The new code specifies that all skirts and shorts must fall no higher than 4 in. above the knee, and shirts must be tucked in. "When one of our teenagers comes in looking like Britney Spears, they carry with them an attitude," says Sushko, who began the year by issuing as many as 40 citations a day for inappropriate dress. Tonya's mother Michelle Steed thinks the school's approach is draconian. "Tonya is making an attempt to go to school, and it's like they are trying to deter her by checking her every day," she says.

The Britney effect is helping fuel a resurgence of school dress codes across the country. In Chicago, where 80% of the public schools have uniforms, Assistant Principal Anastasia Halicki patrols the halls of Stephen F. Gale Elementary School to ensure that skirts don't rise higher than two finger widths above the knee. The majority of girls, of course, know better than to wear their most risque clothes to school. Tube tops are forbidden at Oliver McCracken Middle School in Skokie, Ill., but Sarah Roberts, 11, wears hip huggers and skimpy T shirts on the weekend. Even in the dead of winter, a bulky sweater simply won't do. "Boys just notice if skin is showing," she explains, adding that fourth-grade boys line their lockers with posters of Britney.

"We compare ourselves to Britney," Sarah says, "and most of the time it makes us feel bad because we don't match up." She recalls that the pressure to look good began in fourth grade, when a lot of her peers started worrying about their weight. Now a sixth-grader, Sarah has a formidable collection of lip gloss, nail polish and eye glitter (the only makeup her mother allows her to wear). Yet even she believes there should be limits: she would never wear some of Britney's more daring attire, she says, because "there's a difference between looking cool and looking like a slut."

Mothers who try to control the closet rarely agree with their daughters on what that difference is. Mindful of her own teenage years, spent in halters and hot pants, Sandy Swenson struggles to find tasteful outfits that pass the cool bar for her daughter Kate, 14. But the Houston mother admits she prefers at times to retreat rather than fight over wardrobe. Shavetta McWhorter, a mother of two girls in Canton, Ga., takes a harder line. "I basically tell Asa, 12, 'You have two choices: you can dress like a young lady, or you can dress like a hoochie,'" she says, making clear that since she bankrolls the clothes, the option is purely rhetorical. McWhorter has a tougher time shopping for Jasmine, 7. "It's practically impossible to keep her in clothes that cover her up," she says. "The stores have the same things in her size as they do for Asa—down to the thong bathing suits, even the lingerie. In little-girl sizes, they've got the thigh-high panties and padded bras."

Thanks at least partly to Britney, the marketing of sexy clothes and makeup to prepubescent girls is booming. Rave Girl, a national chain, sells feather boas, leather pants and stretch flares to girls ages 7 and up. "Girls' clothes started get-

Do Videos and Television Teach Kids to Rebel Through Fashion?

'We've had problems with spaghetti straps,' said David Ray, principal of Parker's Prairie Crossing Elementary School, which has a strict dress code. When students show up in inappropriate clothing, teachers explain the dress code and tell them not to wear it to school again. Often, they're puzzled. Why not dress like their favorite music stars?

'I can't really blame the manufacturers,' Ray said. 'What we're hearing is that this is the influence of girls in the media. The Britney Spears look. That seems to have a negative influence in terms of what the kiddos are wearing.'

Exactly, says Golden author David Wann, whose book *Affluenza* examines American preoccupation with materialism and technology. While elementary- and middle-school age children lack what Wann calls 'the money leverage of older kids,' they often pressure parents to buy products they've seen on television and in videos.

ting sexier about two years ago," says Jaime Williams, a manager at a branch outside Chicago. "Basically, everybody wants to be a princess. Not like the ones in fairy tales, but a hot princess like Britney." In Manhattan, designer boutiques like Betwixt and Infinity sell adult labels at adult prices in Alice-in-Wonderland sizes. A pair of Diesel jeans at Betwixt costs $70, and a pony-hair dress at Infinity costs $205. "Age-appropriate behavior is something we've lost sense of," says Joan Jacobs Brumberg, the author of *The Body Project*. "It's appropriate to say to children that you do certain things—like drive, wear makeup—at certain ages. Otherwise, the line between childhood and adulthood will disappear."

Where is that line? When does the game of dress-up, which used to take place at home with Mom's red lipstick, become a worrying reality? Fira Cosmetics claims to target females ages 12 to 28, but girls as young as five are buying such

'When kids see how wildly ecstatic Britney Spears is in her videos, then they want that too, that heightened sense of power, and television tells them that the clothes are the way to get there,' he said. 'TV teaches kids to assemble commodities around themselves to identify who they should be, and to make themselves happy. Even if they're only 6 or 7, they want the sneakers, the suggestive clothes, because that's what the marketers tell them will make them happy. The marketers know the parents don't like the products, so their strategy is calculated to break the parental veto—to make the parents look like real fuddy-duddies, and to play on their guilt.'

The August [2001] issue of *CosmoGirl!* for example, tells its young readers to 'Make everyone wonder, "What ever happened to that nice girl we used to know?"'—a marketing concept that delights its young readers and annoys grownups.

Claire Martin, "Below the Belt? Risque Clothing in Pint Sizes Brings Parental Outrage," *Denver Post*, August 29, 2001.

products as the $12 Special Hits, 10 lip glosses and eye shadows contained in a CD case. "The music scene is driving the young scene," says president Ira Adler, explaining why his company packaged the makeup that way. "Britney and some of the other music groups are bursting with glitter and cosmetics." Kiss Products, a leading manufacturer of artificial nails, has licensed Disney characters like Winnie the Pooh and Mickey Mouse to sell its nail products.

Now five-year-old girls are even getting together for nail and glamour parties, which typically feature manicures and makeup sessions. At a party in New York City last week, Tejashree Gopal, 5, chose pink lipstick and blue eye shadow at the makeup station and then had her nails done in different colors. "I don't usually get to wear makeup," she enthused. "It's like against the rules. But here it's a party, so it's O.K." The caterer, Cozy Wolan, who owns a hair-cutting salon for kids in Manhattan, says demand for her parties is growing. Especially since she began offering a new attraction: a choreographer who teaches the kids Britney's dance moves.

EXAMINING POP CULTURE

Men's Attire as an Indicator of Social Class

The Origins of Men's Suits

William Hamilton

Has the suit become irrelevant in today's more casual workplace? For more than a century, suits have been a traditional part of the American male wardrobe. Today, however, new businesses and clothing fads are threatening the status of this fashion staple. Relaxed office dress codes are making formal attire optional all or part of the week, reducing the association between wearing a suit and being considered a professional. In addition, some younger companies have abandoned suit culture altogether. Software engineers in Silicon Valley, California—the heart of the computer industry—are legendary for favoring T-shirts and jeans.

In this article, author William Hamilton provides a brief history of the suit, noting how current designs are still influenced by earlier lifestyles and activities. For instance, modern suit styles still have their origins in riding apparel; a century ago, suits needed to include flaps and jacket slits to allow the freedom of movement required to ride a horse. Despite this association with riding, Hamilton discusses how suits have always been more ceremonial than functional. William Hamilton is a writer for the *Atlantic Monthly*.

"IT'S HARDEST ON THE OLDER GUYS," THE WELL-tailored captain of an elegant New York restaurant known for the ego-mindful seating of its powerful clientele told me last

■

spring. "They don't know what to wear, and when they try, they just don't look right. Look at Gerald Levin over there—he might as well be carrying a toolbox." Levin is the CEO who sent chills through haberdashery, in January [2000], when he wore khaki trousers and an open-necked shirt to the press conference announcing the merger of his company, Time Warner, with AOL. Levin has scarcely been seen in a necktie since.

Later in the season I stopped by a great Manhattan store to have a look around the men's-suits floor. It was nearly empty of customers, and the ranks of hanging suits brought to mind the terra-cotta army guarding the Emperor's tomb near Xian. Would souls ever come to fill these silent human forms, or was this spectacle archaeological, an awesome and monumental reminder of a bygone age?

"About three months ago there was some concern," said an executive called in by a manager who had been called over by a clerk. "But the whole formal look is definitely coming back now." Evidently, the possibility that we were gazing at an obsolescent inventory made my question about how suits were selling too hot to handle for anyone less than a vice-president. When the executive left, the clerk called my attention to an entering customer, a man in shorts, a backpack, and a baseball cap. This apparent hiker or bird watcher picked up a sleeve to look at the tag. Before closing in on him as delicately as a fisherman stalking a trout, the clerk said, "It was those damn dot-coms that nearly killed us, but now that they've all crashed, we're going to be just fine again."

"We went casual in the nineties," the senior partner of a mighty New York law firm told me. "We had to compete with the dot-coms for the best and the brightest new talent, and not just with money. The dot-coms didn't wear suits. No ties. Comfortable cottons. They looked like a new way to do business. Some of my partners still wear suits. And you know who else does? The women. The young women lawyers all wear these black suits, with pants. I think it's so they won't be mistaken for secretaries. But none of the young guys wear suits anymore. I still wear a shirt and tie under my sweater. And I keep a blazer in my closet for important meetings."

Who would argue against the proposition that the twentieth century went farther, faster, than any before it? Yet despite the spectacular, transmogrifying effects of electricity and tele-phones and rockets and nuclear energy and birth-control pills, men, at least in their most official capacities, wore nearly the same outfit the whole time. My grandfather, a member of Yale's class of 1896, kept a photo scrapbook of his college life. The haircuts, suits, ties, and shoes—even such accessories as sus-penders, cuff links, fountain pens, and little wire eyeglasses—in these old snapshots indicate that a male time traveler from 1896 would not look very unusual on a present-day city side-walk (except, of course, for his look of shocked amazement as he took in contemporary transportation, architecture, and women). But in 1896 a man of 1796, in a tricorn hat, powdered wig, knee breeches, buckled shoes, and frock coat, would have looked like someone on his way to a costume party.

The Roman toga and the mandarin robes of Imperial China covered correct officials for years too, but in compara-tively static worlds that their wearers were trying to keep that way. The modern men's suit, with its pockets and sleeves and trouser legs and lapels and buttons, and flying that pennant of necktie, was devised and rigged for motion, like a sailboat. But it came from the turf, not the surf. That split in the back of the jacket was originally cut to drape over a saddle. The notched lapels can close the front as sleekly as a cavalryman's breast-plate. Trousers, too, were probably first pulled on for horse-back riding. The flying skirts of Alexander the Great's legions could cause riders not only sudden gusts of embarrassment but saddle sores.

When conquest became more administrative than heroic, the suit dismounted and gave orders from behind a desk. The outfit never looked smarter or more urban and organized than it did in the nineteenth century, standing against untailored backdrops of crumbling feudalism and spreading colonialism. In counterpoint to the ancient, often buttonless clothing on peasants and muzhiks and natives and slaves, suits were offi-cers' uniforms of the New Authority.

No Utilitarian Value?

Understandably, such a style of dress would come to the rul-ing classrooms of Yale in 1896—but what kept such caballero wear in vogue for yet another hundred years? Jackets cut for saddles are cumbersome in cars. In our indoor, thermostat-steadied atmospheres the suit and tie can feel as monstrously clumsy as the old lead-footed, copper-domed suits in which deep-sea divers were lowered to the muddy bottom. In fine restaurants many chairs containing males are now hung with removed suit jackets. Pilots wear their jackets only in the airport, to look official and able and in charge (and reminiscent of the sea captains they have superseded). Like Clark Kent's boxy double-breasted suit, which had to be removed, in a phone booth or behind a tree, for Kent to function as Superman, ours have become more a transitory disguise than the clothes in which we actually do our work. Could the suit and tie, like the tuxedo, become an example of special-occasion wear? Maybe even a rental?

"Well, the suit per se has no utilitarian value," the senior law partner told me. "It once had a psychological value, but even then it had no actual function. With guys in shirts and jeans working their computers on Microsoft-style campuses, the appearance of a suit just means somebody from outside the hive has arrived—maybe a banker or a lawyer or a mortician. After you've sat in a couple of meetings with billionaires wearing shorts—and drinking water from baby bottles the whole time, by the way—you wonder which is stranger: these new guys, or you in your suit and tie?"

The first suit came into focus as photography did. Freezing actual instants of light and shade, the camera took all the guessing, exaggeration, and rumor out of fashion news. There for all the boys to see on a magazine page was a photograph of Queen Victoria's heir, the Prince of Wales, off duty in reality, smoking a cigar in Paris, in trousers, a frontally buttoning jacket, and a necktie. So this is what a man who could buy anything wore when he wasn't in the ermine! Photography saw through the hundreds and thousands of formerly opaque miles and layers of class between his off-duty Royal Highness and the ambitious miners' and farmers' and grocers' sons who would change the world. It turned the robes of state into antiques reserved for parade wear. For the first time the everyday plumage of the unpecked apogee of the pecking order was available for popular study. Tailors clipped such pictures to show their clients, who obviously liked the idea of wearing what the Prince of Wales—and J.P. Morgan and Oscar Wilde and Caruso—did on the boulevards. Despite differences in quality, the suits on Kafka, in Prague, and Santos-Dumont, in Rio de Janeiro, and Toulouse-Lautrec, in Paris, were strikingly alike—and not that different from what Grandpa and his schoolmates wore in New Haven or, amazingly, what Big Business (Gerald Levin excepted) still wears, at least to share-holders' meetings. In the 1890s the suit and tie spread through haberdashery like Gutenberg's Bible through Christendom.

When it started, the new look had considerable advantages: it united all its wearers in a single anonymous, international, and interacting commercial urban class—modern man. Playing at being human, possibly giggling Japanese Emperors stuck their divine hands into their first experience of pockets

T-Shirts Replace Suits in Silicon Valley

[The] penchant for dressing down has its origins in Silicon Valley, where back in the early 1980s computer pioneer Hewlett-Packard introduced "casual Fridays" because that was the day all workers, from top management down, went into the warehouse to help package goods for shipment.

Soon the "Jeans Friday" concept spread throughout Silicon Valley, expanding from one day a week to the seven-day week that many people work there. Backed by clever advertising campaigns from Levi's and other casual dress companies, the practice became prevalent across America through the Nineties. In 1992 just 17 per cent of offices in the U.S. allowed workers to wear casual dress five days a week. By 1997 it was 53 per cent. [As of 2000] even the top lawyers' offices in stuffy New York and Washington have trumpeted their conversion to a casual regime. They hope to attract better workers this way, but the casual trend is causing problems of its own.

Many newspapers have taken to publishing style guides for dressing down that instruct people to avoid wearing

as courtiers tied their neckties. Scottish kilties lost a familiar updraft off the floor. Turkish rug dealers found it more awkward to lounge on their goods smoking their hookahs in woolen stovepipe trousers than it had been in the old, voluminous Kublai Khan cavalry–style pants; but the advantages outweighed any possibly estranging unfamiliarity. The suit offered every nineteenth-century man an identity beyond the tribe, the class, even the nation, of his birth. At least from a distance, the suit offered nineteenth-century man a new self.

Fashions, however, change—or anyway they used to. With sighs of relief, women climbed out of the Spanish galleons of nineteenth-century bustles and whalebone corsets into one new look after another. Men demurred. Perhaps because the suit and tie of 1896 were ahead of their time, and photograph-

---

T-shirts, ripped clothing or anything that is too revealing.

This injunction against the T-shirt won't have much effect on the free-spirited souls at the heart of the high-tech world. While Silicon Valley business types feel comfortable in khaki trousers and button-down shirts from Gap, the engineers and programmers who make all the clever stuff are still firmly committed to the simple garment of the American dream, especially if it is adorned with a high-tech logo or two. . . .

[The T-shirt] is the cornerstone of the tech geek's wardrobe and a testament to his lack of dress sense and detachment from the world of materialism. Together with a pair of wrinkled khaki shorts and hiking sandals, the T-shirt is the closest thing engineers have to a uniform. "You're dealing with people who really can't dress themselves by and large," says engineer David Thomas.

There is also the cachet of wearing something that is an anti-status symbol, an outward sign that the wearer doesn't have to conform to suits, pumps or other confining but socially acceptable business wear.

Andy Goldberg, "Wonderful World of the High-Tech T," *Daily Telegraph* (London), May 4, 2000.

ically promoted, and internationally significant, and as flattering as gift wrap on a wide variety of masculine figures, they stayed à la mode. Human males have a tendency to dress defensively. Unlike women, they dress not so much to look fabulous as to look acceptable. Even so, the old horseback-bred suit and tie should have had it by 1950: by then the future had become a vivid popular fantasy. Men seemed certain to appear eventually in sleek synthetic jumpsuits with magic belts they would use to teleport around the universe, taking an occasional pill to satisfy all their dietary needs. Futuristic tales of 1950 did not picture men of 2000 wearing more or less what Sherlock Holmes did.

Media Influences

What kept the suit in style was television. TV changed the visual world as powerfully and profoundly as photography had done before it. Everything on TV looked incredibly new and exciting, even Ed Sullivan in a suit. Little boys lying on the floor watching TV in 1950—and for the next fifty years—were imprinted with the male dress code seen on newscasters, hosts, quizmasters, sportscasters, evangelists, press secretaries, pundits, and even comedians: the coat and tie. For the aging suit, TV was Viagra. When anchormen moored by ties told viewers that Monica Lewinsky had given President Bill Clinton one so that she could see it around his neck when he next appeared on TV, we may have witnessed this totemic accessory's actual climax. Less than two years after this Pirandello/Marshall McLuhan/Danielle Steel moment of medium-message delivery, Gerald Levin, in the process of announcing that Time Warner had been sucked into cyberspace, made no necktie at all look even louder than Monica's notorious Ermenegildo Zegna.

Now it might seem that the eerily private and portable world facing us on our computer screens could drive dress back to loincloths, or at least bathing suits (though telecommuting may mean that you don't have to go out to work, you still have to answer the door). Bringing the world to you but not you to the world, cyberspace is not a dressy place. . . .

"I don't know—I just don't think we should go around here looking like pizza deliverymen," an annoyed forty-year-old investment banker told me, glaring at the door he'd just shut between us and the elegantly paneled lobby in which some of his colleagues wore golf shirts. "Goddamn it, I think we should look like somebody. Somebody in charge."

Menswear executives I interviewed all agreed that this fall will tell the tale. One said, "If the casual look was a trend, the suit will come back. But if this is evolution, it won't." A well-cut vice-president said, "This fall will be the one in which the suit and tie either make a big comeback or become extinct."

Can our great corporations continue half in suits and half in golf wear? How will the future mark off its officers from its enlisted men? Will casual funerals bury the dead in sweaters? Born with photography and regenerated by television, the relic of horsedrawn times may turn out to have been kicked upstairs by the new technology—the same way ermine and embroidered robes were by photography. The suit, if cryogenically preserved in cyberspace, may find a more democratic but equally ceremonial and possibly eternal life.

The Importance of Dressing Like a Gentleman

Jenna Weissman Joselit

As recently as the beginning of the nineteenth century, fashion was not considered an appropriate conversation topic for "all-American" males. This attitude contrasted with another view held by many Americans—that true gentlemen paid attention to the style and care of their clothing. Men were expected to dress neatly and tastefully, while avoiding paying too much attention to their clothes. Starched collars and creased pants—evidence of neatness and care— were a must in any upstanding man's wardrobe.

A shift in thinking occurred in the mid-1920s, when Americans began accepting a more casual attitude toward everyday living and became more interested in outdoor activities. The scientific and medical professions were especially supportive of this shift, encouraging looser, healthier designs. As part of the trend toward casual dress, men began favoring "ready-to-wear" styles—clothes that were mass produced rather than tailor-made on an individual basis. Change came slowly, however, since most men preferred the prestige associated with gentlemanly attire over the comforts of the newer styles. Jenna Weissman Joselit is a visiting professor of American Studies at Princeton. This overview is excerpted from her book, *A Perfect Fit: Clothes, Character, and the Promise of America.*

■

[IN THE 1920S,] WHETHER CAST IN TERMS OF GE-
ology or of ancient history, men's clothing—give or take a detail or two, like pockets—had hardly changed since the inven-
tion of the suit in the 1800s. Men had long ago abandoned frills
and furbelows in favor of what Anne Hollander calls the "standard masculine civil costume," with its strong, clean lines and
absence of ornamentation. The gentleman of yesteryear might
have adorned his person with all manner of gewgaws but the
modern gentleman eschewed them with a vengeance. Frills did
not accord with his sense of responsibility and probity, trust-
worthiness and solidity. Not everyone, of course, thought the
current trend such a good thing. "When men wore satins and
laces and ruffles, being handsome was not the minor accom-
plishment that it is today," editorialized the *New York Times* in
1926. "Except for movie heroes and matinee idols, men nowa-
days scorn the deliberate struggle for beauty." The National
Association of Retail Clothiers and Furnishers, representing
the menswear industry, was quick to agree. Even in the [twen-
tieth century], when dressing well was not a demanding exercise, the average American man, it pointed out, did not take
great pains with his appearance. He tended to buy a new suit
only when his old one wore out. It was high time the common
man discovered the "pleasure of being well-dressed."

Male Attitudes Toward Fashion

But such pleasure often eluded him. Far more inclined to
make light of clothes than to take them seriously, the average
Joe did not reject the idea of gentlemanliness so much as dis-
dain all talk of fashion. Any discussion of what the well-
dressed man ought to wear seemed, according to one rueful
observer, "to occasion raucous mirth in Seattle, Chicago, New
York or New Orleans alike." It made too many red-blooded
American men uncomfortable. Try as they might, America's
moral arbiters found it difficult to convince the man on the
street that "dressing badly" was not a "sign of intellectual su-
periority"; most men chose to believe otherwise. From their
vantage point, not only was it dumb to pay attention to what
one wore, it was foppish or effeminate. As fashion designer
and writer Elizabeth Hawes explained in *Men Can Take It*, her
breezy account of male attire, American men did not concern

themselves too much with clothing lest they be thought "pansies." The "Harvard boys, and the Yale boys and many, many other men and boys all admit it as a factor."

Still, on or off campus, men did care about their clothing; they just didn't talk about it. "If we are honest," said one of their number, "most of us will admit that we admire the meticulously dressed man. His clothes add a certain halo." Rabbi Alexander Kohut of New York no doubt felt that way. The opportunity, every other year, to purchase a new silk-lined frock coat was a much-anticipated event for the rabbi and his family. Proceeding downtown, his wife and children in tow, Rabbi Kohut would lovingly touch the bolts of satin, silk, and wool laid out before him, much like "a musician softly caressing his beloved piano keys." The supple beauty of the fabric, his wife recalled, "beguiled" him. Laymen like Mr. Wolfson, the hero of an S.N. Behrman short story about the middle-class aspirations of immigrant Jews, revered beautiful clothing, too. The president of a little synagogue in Worcester, Massachusetts, Mr. Wolfson is determined to look important, like a real president. Emulating the upper class, he dons a stovepipe silk hat, a Prince Albert coat, and striped trousers, an ensemble lampooned in Yiddish-speaking circles as a *prinz yankel*, to wear to Sabbath services. "The fabulous circumstance," writes Behrman knowingly, is that Mr. Wolfson "owned these garments outright. In this, he was unique in our community, such garments were nearly always hired, and seldom used except for weddings."

O.O. McIntyre, syndicated columnist and man-about-town, couldn't have been more unlike Mr. Wolfson. Yet he shared Wolfson's affinity for clothing. "I really *enjoy* snappy clothes," McIntyre acknowledged. "I have a good time selecting them. They serve in a measure to increase my sense of well-being." Good clothes had done a lot, too, for the once struggling but now prosperous salesman who wrote in the pages of the *American Magazine* of his "sartorial metamorphosis." Chronicling his conversion to clothes, the salesman described how at one point in his life he disapproved mightily of men who paid attention to their attire. "'Spends everything he makes on himself,'" he'd sniff. Gradually, however, it dawned on him that his attitude was benighted: being better dressed and better groomed might bring him the kinds of rewards that had hitherto eluded him. Having seen the light, he purchased a fashionable wardrobe. "In my new clothes I not only felt a different man, I *was* a different man," he confessed. "And I was treated as such."

Gentleman Standards

Ready-to-wear placed gentlemanliness within the reach of men who once inhabited the outer reaches of society, enabling them to subscribe to its tenets and tout its virtues. Scrupulously honoring the "ten commandments of correct dress," salesmen, journalists, and synagogue presidents now placed a premium on uniformity and understatement, sobriety and restraint. They understood that proper gents made sure their clothes "retreated" rather than "obtruded" and that their hats and shoes harmonized rather than clashed. The true gentleman dressed "cheerfully but soberly," avoided "unruly" neckties, and always wore a spotless white shirt, the "badge of the man who knows what to say when the waiter speaks to him in French." The linguistically proficient American gentleman also avoided anything that smacked of conspicuousness, such as the "luridly colored" shirts, loud checks, and gaudy waistcoats fancied by the members of the fast set. Determined not to give "offense" or, for that matter, to look like a swell, he stayed within the bounds of the perennially "correct dress chart," avoiding that which seemed too fashionable. "What man in his senses wants to look like a fashion plate?" Correctness was far more important.

Well-Creased Trousers

Neatness was another prerequisite of gentlemanliness, or so its guardians insisted. The American gentleman took good care of his clothes, making sure not to fling them on the nearest chair upon retiring for the evening but to put them away neatly, using wooden hangers and other modern "contrivances for keeping trousers in order." Ridding his pockets of its bulky contents—of keys, hankies, pipe and pouch, matches, and scraps of paper—lest they stretch his jackets and overcoats out of shape, the well-dressed man put on a fresh pair of celluloid shirt cuffs and collars as often as he changed his underwear, preferably once a day. And he made sure his clothes "rested." The way to prevent one's trousers from getting baggy, advised those knowledgeable about such matters, was to have at least seven different pairs: "a pair of trousers should have six days' rest to one day's work."

It was not enough for a pair of trousers to be well-rested, they had to be sharply creased as well. "Some years ago," reported the pseudonymous "Major of To-day," author of *Clothes and the Man* (1900), "no respectable man would dream of wearing trousers with that crease in them. Why? Because the crease was then the hallmark of the readymade pair of trousers." But times had changed: "The man whose trousers haven't got one is considered almost slovenly." Men were very particular about their creases, confirmed the proprietor of a

Ties and Pop Culture

After World War II, the olive drab of the military years gave way in the late 1940s and 1950s to the euphoria of peacetime prosperity reflected in an explosion of tie colors, ranging from Hawaiian prints to garish hand-painted scenes of bathing beauties on desert islands.

By the late 1950s and early 1960s, however, mainstream culture favored quiet conformity. The conservative gray flannel suit predominated, with its narrow shoulders, thin lapel and skinny dark ties like those worn by President John F. Kennedy. Or by the Beatles when they first came to the United States just 10 weeks after Kennedy was assassinated in November 1963.

In the late 1960s, again reflecting a cultural shift, ties widened and brightened into flower patterns, exotic motifs, peace symbols and messages of love—the commercialization of the youth culture. Many men in that turbulent time of student protests and urban riots permanently discarded ties, rejecting them as symbols of uptightness and conformity.

Sales slumped for a time in the 1970s with the advent of more casual dress styles, notably including the "leisure

cleaning establishment. "A man wants the crease down his trouser leg in perfect alignment between the inside and the outside seam. He wants it with a razor-like edge and he wants it to last forever!"

Social Pressures on Ethnic Dress

Men in search of social acceptance were especially alive to the aesthetics of gentlemanliness. Within the African American community, for instance, dress was a source of both individual and collective pride, an affirmation of dignity. In the wake of Emancipation, black leaders put their faith in the "gospel of civility," in "Chesterfieldian manners" and restrained dress, trusting that a show of fidelity to the strictures of respectability would confer equality or, at the very least, some degree of par-

---

suit," a snug-fitting jacket and pants combination worn with an open-neck shirt.

Narrower neckties made a comeback in the 1980s with traditional patterns and Windsor knots, inspired in part by the conservative political era and style of President Ronald Reagan. The 1990s saw a widening resurgence to 4.5 inches with new variations—cartoon ties, ties with advertising, ties with messages, ties with complicated computer-age designs.

As the century creeps to a close, store counters are stocked with a mix of styles for Christmas buying, which accounts for 20 percent of annual tie sales. This year, darker, deeper colors predominate, and solid-color ties and subdued patterns to match and blend with dark shirts are designed to produce the "minimalist" look.

The current trend toward somber colors represents to Gerald Andersen, executive director of the Neckwear Association of America, the industry trade group, "a reaction to the exuberance of the Nineties and the search for a different look."

John Mathews, "A Twisted History of Neckties," *Washington Post*, December 8, 1999.

ity. Do not "abate, by jot or tittle, your constant endeavor to become and to be gentlemen," counseled Mrs. M.F. Armstrong, author of *Habits and Manners* (1888), a text designed for the students of Virginia's Hampton Normal and Agricultural Institute, urging the men especially to avoid "looking like a dude." At a time when the "penumbra of slavery" still clung to young black men and women, it was important to take great pains with one's appearance, she wrote, holding out the promise that "propriety of deportment on your part will do more than anything else toward securing for you fair and proper treatment from others." A decade later, E.M. Woods sounded a similar refrain in *The Negro in Etiquette: A Novelty* (1899). Gentlemanly behavior had a lot to do with "raising the social and moral standard of the Negro," he wrote. Careful to distinguish among the "foppish fellow . . . overnice about his dress," the ne'er-do-well, and the true gent, his guidebook offered the following pointers: "Boys, don't wear your hats too high nor too low on the forehead, for it savors of the ruffian"; always wear a clean collar; don't oil your hair; and, by all means, avoid "saturating your clothing" with cologne. After all, Woods declared, turning to a higher authority for support, "what did Father Adam and Mother Eve know about cologne?"

Many African American men acted on the advice outlined in these guidebooks and took the promise of gentlemanliness to heart, especially on the Lord's Day. Every Sunday, recalled Kathleen Adams, who grew up in Atlanta during the early 1900s, all the men she knew, from her father to the local storekeepers, outfitted themselves in Prince Albert coats, striped britches, Stetson hats, walking canes, and, come winter, nice gloves. Jelly Roll Morton remembered everyone in his crowd in New Orleans aspiring to own "at least one Sunday suit, because, without that Sunday suit, you didn't have anything." Like their city cousins, the churchgoing men of rural Clairborne County, Mississippi, delighted in their "good, well cared for suits and nice ties and shirts and hats." Some African American men, however, rejected the aesthetic of gentlemanliness and all that it represented. Thumbing their noses at the pretensions of polite white society, they deliberately cut flashy figures in loud suspenders, sharp shoes, brightly colored shirts and scarfs. To them, flashiness spoke of freedom while restraint spoke of repression. Within the African American community, then, clothing alternately proclaimed one's fidelity to or estrangement from middle-class America.

New Trends Emerge

Immigrants also made much of what they wore. Eager to become American, they quickly learned their way around the haberdasher's, prompting journalist Hutchins Hapgood to observe at the turn of the century that immigrant Jewish men had a "keen eye for the right thing in neckties." Others had a keen eye for brightly colored socks and the very latest in collars, from the "standup" model to the "high turndown." According to the *New York Tribune*, the Lower East Side boasted many new arrivals who worked the field of fashion with great energy. With its "sports" (men known for their extravagantly colored socks and ties) and "stiffs" (men known by their collars), immigrant Jewish men clearly did not lack for "artistic taste." Some among them, like the eponymous protagonist of Abraham Cahan's 1917 classic, *The Rise of David Levinsky*, sought to dress more somberly, like a "genteel American." With practice and time, he would eventually get it right, Levinsky assures himself, confident that the "difference between taste and vulgar ostentation was coming slowly, but surely." Fancying himself a gentleman, the immigrant had reason to feel that America was within his grasp: in a country where even the "poorest devil wore a hat and a starched collar," anything was possible. For one newcomer, in fact, nothing better symbolized the wonders of America than his "several suits, many shirts, his patent leather shoes and two or three kinds of hats"; such sentiments come up time and again in accounts of the immigrant experience. Even youngsters, the children of immigrants, were not immune to clothing's allure. In his memoir of growing up, music critic Samuel Chotzinoff, for instance, vividly remembers how "all manner of boys' clothing, including ravishing sailor suits with whistles attached and smart brown knee-length gabardine overcoats," gaily beckoned to him behind the plate-glass windows of local stores, where grown-up clothes were also arrayed "in all their chic and splendor on marvelous, life-sized dummies."

Real-life men, starched, pressed, and neatly encased in suit and somber tie, were ready to take on the world. Not that any-one noticed. In 1909, fifty women were interviewed by *Good Housekeeping* on the subject "His Clothes—As Seen by Her." Everyone agreed that men's clothes were not terribly interest-ing. When all was said and done, they told the magazine, "we have to love a man in spite of his clothes."

Experiments in Fashion by the Scientific Community

By the mid-1920s, this was no longer true. Growing numbers of lawyers, doctors, and college students began to loosen their collars, experiment with color, and, much to the consternation of the National Association of Retail Clothiers and Furnishers, appear publicly in "flapping" trousers. When introduced two years earlier, commented the *New York Times* in 1927, baggy pants were merely a fad; since then, they had become a habit. Inspired by the postwar era's heightened receptivity to new, looser forms of cultural expression and what, in some quarters, was seen as a revolution in manners, "jazz attire" had infil-trated the staid confines of menswear. For the first time in centuries, men were encouraged to free themselves from the "tyranny of starch" and to dress with greater playfulness—and fewer encumbrances.

The medical and scientific communities encouraged such thinking. Men were paying a price for their "senseless garb," warned some of the nation's leading science magazines, draw-ing on the latest physiological research in Germany, Britain, and the United States. Close-fitting garters, scientists discov-ered, "hampered the blood-stream"; trousers "tightly encir-cled the waist," cutting off circulation; and stiff collars throt-tled the neck, causing headaches. Promoting perspiration, "heat stasis," and sluggishness, men's clothing was also found to be needlessly heavy. A German scientist, it was widely re-ported, weighed the clothing of his male assistant and of his wife, only to discover that the man's shoes alone tipped the scales. Closer to home, Dr. Donald Laird of Colgate Univer-sity was widely quoted as saying that while women's fashions had gotten lighter over the years, men's had remained the same. "Men are still wearing the same gross tonnage of clothes as ever," noted the scientist, adding, for good measure, that the average American male tended to wear about a tenth of his body weight in clothes "while a dog carries only about one-fiftieth of his weight in fur." Even skeptics were encouraged to look no further than their local dance hall for proof that men's clothing was not conducive to being fleet of foot. "When we inspect the clothes worn by dancing marathoners, do we wonder that a woman dancer will wear out two or three partners?"

Dress Reform and Men's Clothing

As evidence of menswear's "anomalies" mounted, men were urged to take their cue from women's fashions and to dress "lightly and airily" in loose-fitting trousers and soft collars and to dispense altogether with neckties, which, some men were now prepared to concede, had "no imaginable use whatsoever." W.O. Saunders, a newspaperman from North Carolina, was among them. A staunch believer in the "gospel of lighter clothing," Saunders sauntered down Fifth Avenue one summer day in 1929 clad only in flowing silk pajamas and a jaunty straw hat. The loosely dressed Southerner was intent on instigating a revolt as far-reaching as that of America's short-skirted women by freeing men from the weight of their clothing and, in turn, the shackles of gentlemanliness.

But his crusade went nowhere. Saunders had "dreamed of being photographed, arrested, persecuted, made to languish in jail for his creed," observed *Outlook* magazine. "He was merely photographed." A burning issue for women, dress reform found little support among American men. Their wives and daughters may have welcomed change and entertained multiple notions of womanliness but they themselves held tight to only one way of being in the world: that of the gentleman. Dress reform for men was "unsound," explained *Outlook*, making clear why the American male should not abandon gentlemanliness in favor of some new way of dressing. "Men's clothes are well enough as they are. They are concealing, they have pockets aplenty, they are of material heavy enough to retain a press and refrain from bulging. They are, mostly, dark; therefore, they are inconspicuous and do not show spots. . . . They do not flap, wilt, look funny, or get in the way, at least not much." Those in the upper reaches of society concurred. According to a 1920s survey of the apparel worn by the three hundred best-dressed men in Palm Beach, the citadel of high society, only 1 percent had taken to wearing a soft collar; everyone else preferred to be a "slave to starch" and convention. "The whole issue of the soft collar is much broader than a mere matter of fashion and taste," columnist Heywood Broun observed. "It is an inevitable symbol. Just as woman is apt to change her whole attitude toward life when she bobs her hair, so it is with the man who turns down his collar. Once he has found stimulation in one act of rebellion, he is likely to go further." Little wonder, then, that most men held back. Being a gentleman was worth far more than physical comfort or the contemplation of change.

3

EXAMINING POP CULTURE

Fashion as
a Business

Brand Names and the Decline of Fashion

James B. Twitchell

James B. Twitchell teaches English and advertising at the University of Florida and has written several books about material culture and consumerism. In the following selection he discusses consumer trends and fashion culture. He describes modern fashion in terms of "diffusion theory," which attempts to explain how fashion trends develop and spread.

Twitchell suggests that the advertising technique of branding has made nearly all merchandise potentially fashionable for the mass market. As a result, not just clothes but also goods such as perfume, home furnishings, and even foods are being marketed as "designer" items. High fashion has become popularized, Twitchell maintains, and is no longer the domain of an elite circle of consumers. Twitchell believes that this phenomenon makes designer goods less prestigious and, therefore, contributes to the decline of designer fashion.

ONE OF THE DOMINANT MYTHS OF CONSUMER culture is that we are each separate individuals and we express this separateness by what we choose to buy. We treasure freedom of choice no matter how inappropriate or how mythic. Of course, at the checkout line, branding refutes that notion. While we may think we are freely consuming goods according

■

to individual desire, we are really gathering them in bundles. Or, to be more accurate, while we think we are acting as the result of individual choice we are really passing through stages, "brandscapes," layers of consumption, in which we are creating new, supposedly improved, versions of ourselves. Ironically, the bar codes are on us.

Although we may not recognize how sensitive we are to brand choices in our own lives, we are certainly aware when we watch stereotypes in the mass media. But are the images that we see on television, for instance, accurate? They don't have to be. That's the beauty part. For example, how many members of the audience watching *Beverly Hills, 90210* have directly experienced the lifestyle of an affluent Southern California teenager? So long as fictional choices are congruent with audience expectations, the image groups will be accepted by the audience. As a result, most viewers may now think of the 90210 lifestyle as involving trips to the health spa, wearing midriff-exposing T-shirts, and driving a BMW convertible. One could have as easily been watching *Dallas* or *Cheers*, for the "truth" about a lifestyle category may be less important than its "mass-mediated" image (i.e., its "reality" as conveyed by mass media depictions) and the social connotations it has for the audience/consumer.

As long as the images *fit*, the audience gets the picture. In fact, it is the expectation of, and pleasure in, the formation of an imaginative construct that is the basis of much modern entertainment. Since the plots are redundant, the excitement is discovering how other people use the same branded objects that we too may be able to buy. If we can't buy the exact brand, we can perhaps afford the knock-off. What critics of consumption see as the layering of the repressive hegemony over unformed imaginations is instead the pleasure of fill in the dots. It is how we exercise not just knowledge, but also a sense of shared community. "Can you believe how cool Kelly looked in Dylan's Porsche!?" our daughter asks her school chums the morning after *90210*. . . .

Fashion Culture

We much prefer the word "culture" to "fashion" because we think that culture is somehow enduring and fashion is transient. Culture is "the best that has been thought and said" for all times, and fashion is whatever is being thought and said this week. Or, to extend further: culture is male; fashion female. Culture is English, fashion French. Culture is high, fashion low. Culture is aesthetic, fashion vulgar. Culture me, fashion you.

The image that most people would associate with fashion would be the runway, the so-called catwalk, down which helplessly emaciated and obscenely overpaid women (girls, really) wear the hopelessly expensive follies of often effeminate men. True, this is an aspect of fashion, an aspect as instructive as it is out of date. In the old days when the rich set the tone for fashion, selling your couture to tastemaking bluenoses would allow you to sell the rest of your line as ready-to-wear to the wannabes.

No more. In fact, the runway show and the kind of fashion it implies is now a favorite butt of postmodern ridicule. When Andrew Logan did his "Alternative Miss World" contests in the 1970s and Susanne Bartsch did her "Voguing" balls in the 1980s, one could see that haute couture was being sent up. Now it has been hijacked. Performance "artist" Kembra Pfahler recently dragged herself down the runway with blue-dyed skin, blackened teeth, and bowling balls strapped to her feet. The fashion world was not as much horrified as melancholy. They knew what was going on. And what of the amazing rise of RuPaul and the blasé acceptance of drag as a way to sell accessories (such as M.A.C., a major cosmetics line distributed by Estée Lauder, no less). Clearly, all these subversions show that in the way we live now, the runway literally is a dead end.

Fashion—this kind of haute fashion—is indeed in disarray. To understand why, one need only follow the money. Fortunes are not to be made selling to the rich, but to the middle class, and not to the old but to the young. Kids are the only ones with sufficient disposable time and money to pay attention and be concerned about style. When teenagers control fashion, every fringe—be it hippies, mods, punks, or grunge—is assimilated quicksilver fast into the system. Rich ladies take to the hills. Little wonder that couture has been relegated to the back sections of the newspaper while kidculture is front page. Just look at the average age of the models in *GQ* or *Vogue* today, and look at what activities the models are pretending to be engaged in. Then have a look at what was happening in the pages of *Esquire* or *Harper's Bazaar* back in the 1950s. . . .

A Brief History of Fashion

What made fashioning the self possible was shopping. Shopping depends on a surplus of goods. Machines made surpluses. Essentially this is why fashion really becomes a modern popular concern, an industrial concern. . . . Moralists and preachers of earlier eras had condemned fashion as overreaching individualism. Only royalty was exempt. For them fashion was a function of control. We do this, you don't. Saint John Baptist de la Salle wrote in his seventh-century treatise *Rules of Christian Manners and Civility* that "singularity in dress is ridiculous: in fact, it is generally looked upon as proof that the mind is somewhat deranged." No one today would take such a stand. Fashion is one of the ways we can assert ourselves, fit in, stand out, be rebellious, conform, break loose.

Just as the allure of fashion now drives youth of all classes to the malls of America, the allure of fashion drove the French bourgeoisie to Paris. In fact, it helped create the bourgeoisie. By the early nineteenth century, traditional tailors who had made entire ensembles were giving way to the specialists. There were hat makers, pants makers, jacket makers, and then this whole process was supercharged by the application of machinery that produced specialty items en masse. As clothes stalls grew into fancy-goods stores, and then, in the 1850s, department stores, so new retail innovations followed. In 1852 Le Bon Marché, the first real department store, opened its doors in Paris with fixed prices, free entry, and an increasingly wide choice of goods. For the first time, the ordinary consumer could put different pieces of clothing together, just the way the courtesans did.

The Demimondaine

Along the way, gender got separated from sex, and keeping up with fashion became women's work. If you look at pre-nineteenth-century portrait painting you will see that fashion was clearly the province of men. But then, with the Industrial

Revolution, something happened. To get fashion to "work," a new and very delicate system had to evolve. A fashion class had to be found, willing to show off and even flaunt new style. Today, this is found along the edges of adolescent culture such as with grunge, punk, hip-hop, and the rest. But in the world of our great-grandparents the role of being daring was played by the demimondaine. She was the "other woman," the younger, sexier, risk-taking woman who would become institutionalized as the mistress. Named after a character in a play of the same name by the younger Alexander Dumas, the demimondaine was a keystone in the fashion industry. Immoral, flashy, given to display, and deeply conscious of money, she was the perfect clotheshorse. On her shapely back, fads could be fashioned, styles made manifest, and shopping for a style could begin in earnest.

The demimondaine, not the couturiers, made Paris the fashion capital of the world. Without her, "women of refinement," who have always been slightly afraid of the demands of fashion, could not know what was vulgar, aka exciting, aka sexy. From here the iron rule of modern fashion evolved: what fashion abhors as vulgarity today becomes stylish tomorrow. And one step further, in Oscar Wilde's elegant expansion, "It is only the modern that ever becomes old-fashioned."

Ironically, perhaps, the dressing of these young women made the first designer brandnames as haute couture was born. Without them, and their sense of changing styles, Monsieurs Boucicaut, Cognacq, and Jaluzot, respectively the founders of Bon Marche, Samaritaine, and Printemps, could never have succeeded with the merchandising of a never-ending flow of shifting styles. Retailers did not create desire, however comforting it may be to think, but they certainly harvested it.

The Design as Brand: Suit Up

Fashion messages used to come in nice complementary branded packages. You can still see the aura of this earlier world in the desire of Gucci (and his customers) to stamp his G, or Chanel her C, or Ralph Lauren his tiny polo player, or Lacoste his alligator. Like a work of poetry, fashion accessories rhymed. The shoes rhymed with the belt, the blouse with the scarf, the skirt with the jacket, and so on. In the modern world of television, you just connect the dots. You try to line up the Gs, Cs, polo players, or alligators and, voilà, you are set to go out in style.

This was called a look, as in Dior's "New Look," for instance. For a decade after World War II, Dior reigned over the world of fashion with emphatically tiny waists and vast and sumptuous full skirts. I grew up looking at these clothes. Now they are at the Met. They still inspire vehement, even militant, pleasure or horror. They are so controlled and coherent and unlike anything you see around us now. They do indeed seem built, as the designer Geoffrey Beene has said, to transform female torsos into pedestals. If you look at advertising of the 1950s you can see that not only were women looking *like* pedestals, they were often pictured *on* pedestals.

Dior's dresses were suits of armor. The male counterpart was the gray flannel suit. This uniform hung around for years covering Cary Grant and becoming a metaphor of ambiguous conformity with the film, *The Man in the Gray Flannel Suit.* Sold at Brooks Brothers, Paul Stuart, and J. Press, it gave Madison Avenue a bad name. We now use the word "suits" as a metonym of scorn. Yet, a generation ago, when fashion was still coherent, the suit was king. You wanted to wear one. I remember my first suit. Although my mother took me to buy pants and sport coats, my father took time off from the office to buy me the suit. Say what you will, the suit caught a postwar longing to reassert control. It was a return to tradition and enduring values. Suit up. No dress-down Fridays. Men in black (or at least gray). Suiting was serious and so rebelling against it was almost preordained. . . .

In the last [quarter of the twentieth century,] the power of commercial branding has rapidly moved outward from the face (Cover Girl cosmetics to make you into the literal cover image of a fashion magazine), to the body (Maidenform, body by Jake), to the choice of vehicle (the Bill Blass edition of the Lincoln, the Eddie Bauer Jeep), and now even to the inside of the house (Martha Stewart and Ralph Lauren both have lines of designer house paint). A generation ago few people knew the names of interior designers. Yet today the names of Martha Stewart, Laura Ashley, and Ralph Lauren are like next-door neighbors. In fact, entire "looks" of branded design stuff can give your house a unique personality, to match your own.

Take an abstract concept, for instance, like homeyness. The progenitor of the homey is the English country home. This look has recently taken on aspects of a franchise, complete with numerous accessories. We all know it by heart. Homey is warm (orange, gold, green, brown); physical (wood, stone, brick, nothing plastic please); detailed (bay windows, beamed ceilings, dark wainscotting, joyful fireplaces, shutters, porches, small paned windows, small front door); fabricked (floral); furnished (in wood only) and filled with paddywhack images of personal significance (silver framed pictures of family and pets, tattered books).

How "Homeyness" Is Constructed

Just look at the ads in *The New Yorker* or the *New York Times Magazine*. Homey is on every other page. The English home look is informal, cluttered, humble, comfy, unpretentious, reassuring, riskless. Every form moves inward to the secure and successful and protected self: low ceilings, small windows, ivy on outside walls, magazines on tables, overhanging roof, awnings, hardback books, reading lights, circles of chairs—warm and comfy. You can almost scratch and sniff this look. It smells of good cooking. You can almost taste it. What is that smell? Is it bread, coffee, or bacon cooking? No, it's Thanksgiving turkey.

Homeyness is a cultural construction and, as such, it can be prefabricated and then merchandised. Home sweet home is now as easy to construct as is the family crest. You send in your check and you receive by return mail a coat of arms. Laura Ashley or Ralph Lauren can assemble it, bric by bric, giving you either the feminine or masculine flavor. Generating this look is the basis of retail empires.

Just take a walk up Madison Avenue and look in the shop windows. Interior house design is just an extension of exterior body display. So here we have the elegant shops of Ralph Lauren, Calvin Klein, Versace, Armani, Joseph, and even Gucci that carry everything from clothing to glassware. Fashion plays no favorites, however. What was once the preserve of the clients of "Sister" Parish (1910–1994), doyenne of English-style decorators in America, is now available down at your local Ethan Allen furniture store and is being delivered by the truckload stamped with the Martha Stewart name down at Kmart. . . .

Seinfeld and Diffusion Theory

Clearly what is happening is that fashion is up for grabs. In the eighteenth century, fashion flowed from the court to the courtesans; then in the nineteenth century from the designers to the demimondaine; now fashion is flowing from all over, especially up from the street. The only truths that have remained constant are that imputing *intent* to fashion is a tricky business, and that while fashion may be a visual art, and while it may be deep social commentary, it is primarily a way to manufacture difference and to sell new stuff. Just as movie makers make movies to make money, fashion designers make clothing for much the same reason. Call them auteurs if you want, call them couturiers if you must, but if they want to succeed they need to be called credit worthy by their bankers.

The great shift in fashion is how style is spread around. Let's return to my favorite text of modern consciousness, [the television sensation] *Seinfeld*. On October 6, 1994, an episode titled "The Pledge" focused on the subject of the communication of style, fad, and fashion. Elaine sees the insufferably pompous Mr. Pitt eating a Snickers bar with his fork. She tells curious George, who then casually uses his silverware to eat candy in the Yankees board room. Soon Yankee execs are using their forks, then the players start doing it, and finally, full circle, at Monk's Cafe, the coffee shop hangout, Elaine sees everyone eating Almond Joys with knives and M&Ms with spoons. She yells out: "What's the matter with you people. Are you mad?"

They are not, of course. They are simply participating in what is known as "diffusion theory." How are things adopted as standards? How is etiquette communicated? How do we know what to say, wear, behave? How does fashion flow? The first scholarly research centered on not candy in Manhattan or clothing in Paris but hybrid seed corn in Greene County, Iowa. In the 1930s a superior corn was available but not adopted by any of the 250 farmers in the county. Only a few planted it in 1933; then in 1934 there were 16; then 25, then 21 more; in the next year 36; and the following year 61. After that the rate of acceptance dwindled—46, 14, three, until by 1941 all but two farmers studied were using new seed. No one knows why the diffusion works in this balloon-like bell curve, but it does.

The Fashion Creators

Marketers claim to be able to isolate various groups calling them, by turns, Innovators, Early Adopters, Early Majority, Late Majority, and finally, the Laggards. The entire process is sometimes called trickle down, but that does not account for the systolic pulse that moves like a rabbit through the python. There is nothing new about the process. Supposedly, Josiah Wedgwood used this emulation-based technique when launching his china in the 1750s. First supply the fashion leaders, in this case, the crowned heads of Europe, and the inexorable inflating of the fashion bubble will occur. Sometimes the names of the consumption clusters change, but the inflation-deflation pulse remains constant.

Each broad social group, the theory goes, will have—now in hipper lingo—Purists, a handful of people who create the fashion; Style Leaders, who pick up on it first; Early Adaptors, who crave recognition by the Style Leaders; Happy Compromisers, who know they're not Style Leaders but know what's "in" and what they want from it; and the Unsophisticated, who dress up, dress funky, but probably get things six months too late. In the seed corn scenario made urban, these latecomers— fresh from the farm, as it were—can only watch as one bandwagon after another goes over the horizon. . . .

The T-Shirt as Example

Consider the humble T-shirt. Two generations ago it was part of the working-class uniform. Who can forget the uproar following Clark Gable's epochal unveiling in *It Happened One Night* (1934). He was *not* wearing an undershirt. How daring! But even worse was that by the 1950s the T-shirt started to hang around with the wrong crowd. It became the uniform of the anxious adolescent outlaw, worn by sensitive hoods and motorcyclists (Marlon Brando in the 1953 film *The Wild One* and James Dean in *Rebel Without a Cause*), usually accessorized with a dangling cigarette and a leather jacket. How dangerous!

When Tennessee Williams's play, *A Streetcar Named Desire*, premiered in New York City, Marlon Brando's white T-shirt took top billing.

The T was next appropriated by the hippies. With bell-bottom pants and tie-dyed Ts, they offered another brand of anarchy. Not long after, T-shirts were catapulted to high style by the likes of Jackie Kennedy Onassis, who was spotted wearing T-shirts during the 1970s. Diffusion theory taking hold. By the 1980s, Don Johnson put T-shirts into the male mainstream of style when he sported them with jackets on *Miami Vice*. In a generation the short-sleeved cotton undershirt had gone from extreme hot to extreme cool.

The T-shirt is an apt example of how branding works with fashion once the fashion bubble is inflated. While the T-shirt never lost its democratic flair, designers understood its allure. In the words of Giorgio Armani: "Under a T-shirt, the beautiful bust of a woman or the handsome chest of a man are sculpted and desirable without becoming vulgar." He continues, writing in the Introduction to *The White T*, "And then, I love the T-shirt as an anti-status symbol, putting rich and poor on the same level in a sheath of white cotton that cancels the distinctions of caste." Given such an observation, it was inevitable that designers would attempt to brand the object with their emblematic stamp—the T-shirt with the interlocking C and K, or the Polo pony, or DKNY.

Blue Jeans: The Origins of a Fashion Institution

Doris C. Williams

Blue jeans are regarded the world over as an "American" trademark. Once strictly work pants, jeans have become appropriate city, campus, and even office attire. In this article, author Doris C. Williams provides a chronological history of Levi's—the company that pioneered blue jeans with its "501" brand. Dutch immigrant Levi Strauss introduced the heavy work pants during the California gold rush as a solution for miners who kept tearing their lightweight clothing, but only after World War II did blue jeans become a staple of American fashion.

A FORMULA FOR SUCCESS: COMBINE DEMAND, INgenuity, and vision. Blend in a few well-placed copper rivets, some indigo dye, and a length of heavy *serge de Nimes* fabric. Collect all of the above in San Francisco and assemble under the supervision of a Latvian tailor. Add the financing and marketing genius of a Bavarian entrepreneur, and you have the first pair of Levi's Patent Riveted 501 Waist High Overalls.

In 1848, an event at Sutter's sawmill, 50 miles east of Sacramento, sent a shock wave surging through the California Territory and radiating across the continent. Reports of a Scottish carpenter's discovery of gold traveled eastward by word of mouth, letter, and newspaper to the port cities of New York, Boston, and Norfolk. News of the mother lode, a strip

■

From "Those Pants of Levi's: A Great Western Enterprise," by Doris C. Williams, *Journal of the West*, 1997. Copyright © 1997 by *Journal of the West*. Reprinted with permission.

of land over 100 miles long, also funneled through the Midwest to the frontier states of Ohio and Missouri.

Levi Strauss Leaves St. Louis

In St. Louis, a Jewish peddler named David Stern and his wife Fanny, sister of Levi Strauss, heard of the gold strikes. They saw as their golden opportunity not the struggle for shiny bits of metal, but the sale of dry goods to newly prosperous California folk. The Sterns, taking with them a large quantity of merchandise, joined a wagon train heading West. They planned to open a small dry goods business in what would become a town of 35,000 people. The town, called Yerba Buena under Mexican rule, by 1851 would be known as San Francisco.

In December 1848, as the Nation's capital confirmed the gold strike, 19-year-old Levi Strauss traveled to the rugged and sparsely populated state of Kentucky. His brothers, Jonas and Louis, established dry goods merchants in New York, furnished their younger sibling with a peddler's pack, sending him on his way with thread, yard goods, needles, combs, scissors, razors, and perfume, items offered by traveling salesmen to rural families.

Levi Strauss traveled alone, as did most peddlers of that time, often walking ten or more miles each day. If he was fortunate, when darkness fell he found shelter in barns or sheds along the route. He worked diligently, dealing fairly with those who bought goods from him, establishing, even at a young age, the attitude and model for his future: perseverance and commitment to ethical business practices.

In 1853, determination was a prerequisite for any stout-hearted soul taking passage on a clipper ship. At David and Fanny Stern's urging, Levi booked passage on just such a ship bound for California. Anticipating the needs of fellow passengers, he determined to profit immediately from the trip. As the Sterns had done before him, Levi loaded himself down with assorted merchandise, including brown canvas tent fabric. On March 14, 1853, after sailing down the Eastern coast, around the tip of South America, and through the Straits of Magellan, a journey of 17,000 miles, the clipper ship dropped anchor in California. When Levi Strauss stepped off the ship in the rowdy city of San Francisco, the brown tent canvas was all of his goods that remained unsold. Very soon, the ingenious peddler would sell that, too.

Arrival at the Mines

Thousands of adventurous souls had made their way toward Sutter's Mill. Driven by visions of incalculable riches, they had suffered the severe hardships of scorching desert sands, bone-chilling cold in the mountain passes, torrential rains, cholera and dysentery, and clashes with Indians. Much has been said for the travelers: their endurance, their unwavering determination, and their willingness to sacrifice. The individuals, however, held up much better than their clothing. For Levi Strauss, the first element in the formula for success presented itself: demand.

Levi possessed within himself the second component: ingenuity. Upgraded from carrying a pack on his back to traveling by wagon, he rambled throughout the mining camps. Anxious to provide miners and prospectors with needed goods, he noted with interest their complaints regarding the shoddy quality of their pants: "Pants don't wear worth a hoot in the diggin's!"

Levi took his brown tent canvas to a tailor who produced the first pair of "jeans," a term applied to pants worn by Genoan sailors. Soon Levi had orders for so many pants that the supply of canvas was depleted. In replenishing his stock of cloth, he switched to a more substantial fabric originating in Nimes, France, called *serge de Nimes*, which later became known simply as "denim." With the introduction of synthetic indigo dye, the brown cloth that had been used to sew thousands of pants was replaced by the deep blue denim we know today.

Establishing a Business

In the 1860s, Levi abandoned the trappings of a peddler. He and David Stern left the retail business behind, establishing themselves as one of San Francisco's more prosperous purveyors of wholesale dry goods. European imports such as Belgian lace, hats, shirts, and fine Irish linens, forwarded to them by brothers Jonas and Louis who had remained in New York, graced the pages of their catalogues.

By 1866, a splendid new building on Battery Street housed Levi Strauss & Company, comprised of Levi, the driving force behind the organization, David Stern, Jonas and Louis Strauss, and Levi's oldest sister's husband, William Sahlein. Ten salesmen, covering California and the neighboring states, contributed to the annual sales of $3 million.

In 1872, Jacob Davis, a Latvian tailor and customer living in Reno, Nevada, wrote to Levi Strauss, detailing his own method for sewing work pants, attaching the pockets with copper rivets formerly used on tents.

> . . . I wish to make you a Proposition that you should take out the Latters Patent in my name as I am the inventor of it, the expense of it will be about $68, all complit [sic]. . .

Back in San Francisco, Strauss understood the meaning of the letter in spite of the poor spelling. The following year, United States Patent #139,121 issued jointly to Jacob Davis and Levi Strauss & Co. read:

> As a new article of manufacture, a pair of pantaloons having the pocket openings secured at each edge by means of rivets whereby the seams at the points named are prevented from ripping, as set forth.

One month after the issuance of the patent, the company sold its first pair of denim overalls. Levi disliked the term jeans, and insisted they be designated "waist overalls."

Development of an Industry

Another factor in the formula for success—vision—became reality as Levi installed 60 sewing machines in a building on Fremont Street and hired 60 women operators. With Jacob Davis as head tailor, Levi Strauss & Co. took another step forward. By the end of 1873, miners, cowboys, lumberjacks, and other workers throughout the West had purchased 21,600 pants and hunting coats with riveted pockets.

As the 20th century approached, Levi Strauss & Co. continued expanding, motivated once again by the indispensable elements of its foundation: demand, ingenuity, and vision. At the turn of the century, the factory employed 250 people sewing the distinctive pants, standardized into two lines—off-white or tan duck, and 9-ounce indigo-dyed blue denim. Orange stitching, the signature rivets, and a sewn-on leather label guaranteeing a "new pair free" if the product ripped, set these pants apart from competing products. Assigned the designation of Lot #501, the indigo pants featured a trademark motif stitched in orange thread on the back pocket. Resembling the wings of a bird in flight, the arcuate design is still in use today, the oldest apparel trademark on record.

Levi Strauss died in 1902. Never having married, he entrusted the company to his four nephews. In addition to the tangible evidence of his success, he left the abundant legacy of an honorable life. On the day of his death, the San Francisco *Call*'s headline put it best:

> His life [was] devoted not only to fostering the highest commercial conditions, but to moral, social and educational welfare and development of the young men and women of the State.

He had established 28 scholarships at the University of California and had made numerous bequests to orphanages and various benevolent organizations.

The years following the founder's passing were more difficult for Levi Strauss & Co. The 1906 San Francisco earthquake turned the company headquarters into a pile of rubble and brought production to a standstill.

Uncle Levi would have taken great pleasure in knowing of the nephews' decision to continue to pay employees' salaries immediately following the earthquake and during the construction of a new six-story "wholesale store" on Battery Street and a half-block long factory on Valencia Street. The concept of "family" set in motion by Levi himself is carried on today, yielding fruits of employee loyalty and strong working relationships.

Levi's in the Twentieth Century

The pants, with very minor exceptions, have maintained the same design since their introduction in 1873. Marketing of waist-high overalls was for years confined to the West, where sales figures peaked and could rise no higher. Despite introduction of a line of children's overalls, profits remained small. In 1921, after 50 years of service as Levi's successor, Jacob Stern retired, passing the presidency to his brother, Sigmund. At that time, there was talk among the partners of selling the operation. Sigmund Stern prevailed upon his son-in-law, Walter Haas, Sr., to join the firm. The 30-year-old Haas immediately brought the bookkeeping system in line with the times. He increased the advertising budget to further his goal of introducing the entire country to the Levi's brand. He then convinced his brother-in-law, Daniel Koshland, to abandon the securities business in New York City and come West.

In 1928, Haas became the company's president with Koshland second in command. Walter Haas's interest in finance and marketing and Daniel Koshland's involvement in production and personnel held the organization together throughout the Great Depression in spite of declining sales and mounting inventories.

A New Clientele

Then change swept across the land. In the aftermath of the Depression, Western cattlemen dubbed their operations "dude ranches" and opened them to vacationing Easterners. Upon returning to the East, many of the visitors began to adopt the relaxed style of Western clothing, demanding that sophisticated stores like Abercrombie & Fitch provide them with the same pants cowboys wore. In addition, reel after reel of Western movies spinning out of Hollywood drew attention to the actors' clothing. Walter Haas took advantage of this trend. Incorporating the Western theme into his advertising, he secured forever a direct association between the sturdy, riveted pants and the rugged, adventurous spirit of the American West. Walter Haas, Sr., stated,

> It was a combination of luck, opportunity and imagination, and really, our advertising people [who] put a certain imagination into the waist overall.

In the 60 years following the introduction of waist-high overalls, the pants had seemed best identified with workmen, miners, logging mill hands, and farmers. Then, in addition to being associated with cowboys, West Coast college students adopted them as a status symbol, referring to them as "Levi's." Executives on Battery Street realized that not only had they tapped into a vast market, but they had acquired a new trademark as well.

With the advent of World War II, the denim pants with

their robust reputation became part of a lengthy list of commodities essential to the U.S. war effort. Before awarding contracts to Levi Strauss & Co., however, the War Production Board requested several changes in the pants: rivets would come off the watch pocket, and the famous arcuate design, considered then no more than a decorative use of thread, would be painted on. Levi Strauss & Co. built three new factories to implement these profitable contracts.

The Postwar Jean Craze

After the war, the fascination with Levi's caught on around the world via personnel in occupying forces who wore them when off duty. In Europe, all things "American" became must-haves for the youth. Levi's were a status symbol, a statement of escape from the dreary and dowdy postwar milieu surrounding the rebuilding. Although less expensive knock-offs were available to them, young people wanted the real thing; they wanted Levi's. Levi's became highly desirable black-market items.

Soon demand eclipsed production capabilities, and thus in 1948, Levi Strauss & Co. abandoned dry goods wholesaling to focus entirely on the manufacture of its own products. That same year, and for the first time ever, company profits exceeded $1 million.

In the 1950s, the movie industry once again helped promote the popularity of Levi's, just as it had 20 years earlier. In *The Wild Ones*, a Levi-clad Marlon Brando sat defiantly astride his motorcycle, and James Dean, a sullen symbol of rebellion in rumpled Levi's, shuffled languidly across the screen in *East of Eden* and *Rebel Without a Cause*.

Levi Strauss & Co. introduced numerous design changes during the 1960s: jeans became more tapered, pre-shrunk jeans made their debut, and garments of corduroy and polyester along with White Levis® entered the marketplace, affirming the company's ability to keep pace with fashion trends. But it was the traditional blue denim worn by Brando and Dean that became the uniform for the '60s Beat generation—the Beatniks, and for civil rights workers, Peace Corps volunteers, rock and roll bands, and Vietnam protest marchers.

In 1965, as a result of phenomenal growth, executives at Levi Strauss & Co. established international divisions in Europe and Asia. By 1992, the latest year for which international figures are available, these divisions contributed a 53 percent share of the company's $361 million profits.

New Personnel and New Missions

Enter the '70s. The new decade called for updating garment design as well as major corporate changes. Under Peter Haas, who had succeeded brother Walter as president, continued growth in dollar volume, variety, and geographic considerations which strained the company's concept of organization by line. A new organizational chart replaced the old, with marketing "divisionalized." Under the new system, an executive vice president's responsibility consisted of eight operating divisions: marketing, personnel, four product divisions, LS International and the Canadian G.W.G. Co.

Since its beginning, the company had financed capital improvements with short-term loans and internal sources, but the volume of business in the 1970s demanded infusion of large amounts of capital for plant construction as well as other aspects of business. In 1971, for the first time, the family decided to offer stock to the public. A short four years later, sales hit the $1 billion mark and then doubled in 1979.

Besides doubling its own sales record in the exhilarating decade we remember as the '70s, another type of growth took place at Levi Strauss & Co. that was unique to industry at that time. An awareness of social responsibility and community obligations led to the creation of the Community Affairs Department and Community Involvement Teams. In the tradition of founder Levi Strauss, employee volunteers donated time and money to local projects ranging from day-care centers to the creation of employment for low-income citizens.

In 1981, the first non-family president, Robert Grohman, assumed the position of leadership at Levi Strauss & Co., by then the world's largest apparel company. Over 100 factories, warehouses, and sales offices spread across the U.S. and beyond with annual sales upwards of $2.5 billion.

The company continued to reach milestones throughout the '80s: Levi's Plaza, a few blocks removed from the original site, opened in 1981. Levi Strauss & Co. was designated official outfitter of the 1984 U.S. Olympic winter and summer teams as well as the Los Angeles Olympic Staff. Walter Haas, Sr., company president in the troublesome '30s, had realized then the invaluable power of advertising. Continuing that practice, a new president, Robert Haas, grandson of Walter, Sr., launched the largest single product ad campaign in history, for "Levi's 501 Blues," telecast during the 1984 Summer Olympics.

The following year, Haas led a successful effort to repurchase publicly owned stock, thereby restoring full ownership of the company to the family. Under young Haas's leadership, in 1986, the Dockers® line was introduced, said by some to be the fastest growing brand in the history of the apparel industry. Dockers® alone, now 30 percent of Levi's U.S. sales, is a billion-dollar-plus business with nearly 7 in 10 American men owning at least one pair. If Dockers® was a company unto itself, it would be the sixth largest in the apparel industry.

By the end of the '80s, Levi Strauss & Co. boasted an impressive statistic: between 1853 and 1989 more than two billion pair of jeans had been sold.

Growth in the Nineties

To use jargon of the '90s, Bob Haas, now CEO and chairman of the board, has succeeded in heightening the manufacturing giant's awareness. The world's largest apparel manufacturer is revamping its entire operation with reorganization beginning on the factory floors and extending throughout the hierarchy. All 37 North American factories are switching from the assembly-line method, in which a worker performs one task repetitively, to teams of cross-trained operators who produce garments from start to finish.

Conflict resolution, ethical awareness, empowerment, diversity, and new behaviors are terms with which all 34,000 employees, through training seminars, will ultimately be conversant.

Looking toward the 21st century, Levi Strauss & Co.'s mission statement asserts:

> When we describe the kind of LS&Co we want in the future what we are talking about is building on the foundation we have inherited: affirming the best of our Company's traditions, closing gaps that may exist between principles and practices and updating some of our values to reflect contemporary circumstances.

With 40,000 retail outlets in 70 countries, the company, never static, plans to open 300 Levi's specialty stores by 1998, and after that another 300 if all goes well. The popular Levi's 501 is still the number one choice around the world. Threadbare 501s, often purchased for $5 from Montana cowboys, make the trip to the boutiques of New York City, where they are offered in all their faded glory. With pockets worn thin by snuff tins, and rips and tears inflicted by barbed wire, the 501s still command $75 or more a pair.

Levi's are a part of history—their story reflective of a hearty determination and a lasting spirit, the spirit of the American West.

Helmut Lang: Breaking the Rules of the Fashion Industry

John Seabrook

Helmut Lang was born in Austria but has become an influential force in the American fashion world. His simple yet stylish designs epitomize the "new casual" outfit popular in the 1990s, a look which has become the dress code for many workplaces. Along with impacting clothing design—the end result of the fashion industry—Lang's success and personality is promoting American fashion manufacturers themselves. Lang, along with colleagues such as Ralph Lauren and Donna Karan, has turned fashion designers into public figures. Indeed, part of this fame is related to the new, more visible relationships between movie stars, musicians, and sports figures and designer clothing.

This article offers a glimpse into Helmut Lang's fashion philosophy and his professional and personal influence on the American fashion community. Author John Seabrook is a freelance journalist and staff writer for the *New Yorker*, where this article was originally published.

ABOUT FOUR YEARS AGO, IN A MEN'S STORE called Camouflage, in Chelsea [a neighborhood in New York

Excerpted from "The Invisible Designer: Can Helmut Lang Become a Brand Name and Still Retain His Mystique?" by John Seabrook, *The New Yorker*, September 18, 2000. Copyright © 2000 by Condé Nast Publications, Inc. Reprinted with permission.

City], I tried on some trousers. They were perfectly ordinary-looking thin-wale corduroys, and yet something about them was different: the fabric was softer, the color was slightly subtler than basic black. The pants were unpleated, the rise was high, the leg slim. There was a loop for the button over the rear pocket, and an inner waist button—details you don't often find on sportswear. Was this fashion? Perhaps, but it was hidden; only I would know. The label was inside, too, small and not at all logomaniacal—just the words "Helmut Lang" in black on white. It seemed intended to evoke the "tickets" you find inside bespoke suits from made-to-measure tailors. The pants cost a hundred and twenty dollars—not bad, as designer clothes go. I bought them.

This encounter occurred during my quest to shed the preppy uniforms I'd been wearing in the fifteen years since college—a tux for formal occasions, a suit for church and funerals, a blue blazer and tailored slacks for looking "smart," a polo shirt and khakis for going out on weekends—and to find a more casual style, one that was better suited to the identity I was imagining for myself. (Clothes, of course, are not so much about who you are as who you want to be.) I had discovered the melancholy truth that men everywhere have learned as they try to master the new casual style at the office: dressing casually actually requires that a man take fashion more seriously than dressing formally does. The new casual, like the old casual, is supposed to give an appearance of ease, of comfort with yourself. But, unlike the old casual, the new casual is all about status. "Casual Power," a recent style guide by Sherry Maysonave, describes a hierarchy with six different levels of casual attire: Active Casual, Rugged Casual (also called "outdoorsy"), Sporty Casual, Smart Casual (or "snappy"), Dressy Casual, and Business Casual. This may be the most depressing thing about the casual movement: no clothing is casual anymore.

Helmut Lang, the Austrian-born designer, seemed to understand exactly what I needed—a uniform for the new casual world. I bought some more of his clothes: a ribbed cotton sweater that didn't stretch like my other cotton sweaters; a few pairs of khakis, which had a pleasingly crisp finish; a denim shirt; a woollen sweater in a beautiful straw color; and a pair of jeans. They were intelligent clothes, designed for a maximum number of situations, both work and play, which increasingly seem to be performed in the same outfits.

But there was also a deceptive aspect to my new uniforms. They appeared to be casual, but they were not, and I knew they weren't. The designer seemed to be playing off this stealthy quality by hiding certain nonfunctional fashion elements inside the clothes, such as the faux drawstrings inside the waistband of otherwise totally ordinary chinos. This hidden streak extends to the way the clothes are presented. The Helmut Lang store in SoHo, which was designed in close collaboration with Richard Gluckman, a New York–based architect of galleries and museums, violates the most basic principle of retail design: you are supposed to be able to see the merchandise. Here the clothes are concealed from view when you walk in—enclosed inside alcoves in the middle of the store. Hiding, it seems, is part of who Helmut Lang is.

Lang and the American Fashion Awards

Hoping for a glimpse of the man whose name was inside my clothes, I attended [the 2000] American Fashion Awards, which took place at Lincoln Center in June. Polly Mellen, a longtime arbiter of American fashion, was at a buffet supper preceding the awards, scanning the big white tent for that sleek, seal-like shape that she said she found so enchanting—Helmut Lang's head. "Where are you, Helmut, where are you?" she called out. "You are our glamour boy. You have to come."

Lang . . . had been nominated for all three of the evening's major awards—for womenswear, menswear, and accessories—an honor never before bestowed on any designer. He moved his business from Paris to New York in 1997, and this spring he joined the Council of Fashion Designers of America. The C.F.D.A., which organized the awards ceremony, was happy to count as one of its own the designer whose utilitarian, austere, sportswear-inspired aesthetic was widely copied during the nineties, and became the dominant style of the decade: minimalism. These honors were a way of recognizing his influence, which is likely to increase—Lang recently formed a partnership with the Prada Group—as well as a way of welcoming him to the club.

[Designer] Tommy Hilfiger was in the tent, shaking hands

and flashing his toothy, sideways grin. Chloe Sevigny came in wearing a Helmut Lang organza skirt. Elizabeth Hurley and Claudia Schiffer appeared, looking very eighties, both in gorgeous, shimmery Valentino gowns with ruffles around the bosom. There is nothing restrained about Valentino—elegance and beauty come before comfort and function. "Too fussy," pronounced Polly Mellen, continuing her search for Helmut Lang.

But Lang was nowhere to be found. It seemed he had decided to stay in his SoHo headquarters, where he was working on his spring, 2001, menswear collection. (Fern Mallis, the C.F.D.A.'s executive director, received word from Lang's P.R. agency about an hour before the event began, and said she was "flabbergasted.") As the news spread that Lang was not going to appear at the party, the festive spirit began to leak out of the tent. There was a feeling that Lang might not want to be a member of the club, after all.

A Strained Relationship with the Fashion Community

Lang lost the first big award of the evening, Accessory Designer of the Year, which went to the team of Richard Lambertson and John Truex. But he won the next one—Menswear Designer of the Year. When his name was announced, many in the audience, not yet aware of his absence, expected a rare sighting of the man himself, and there was an audible groan as Ingrid Sischy, the editor-in-chief of *Interview*, appeared out of the darkness and mounted the podium, where she solemnly accepted the award for Lang, whom she thanked for "changing the rules in American fashion." The line did not go over well with the crowd, which included most of the rulemakers. (Cathy Horyn, the *Times* fashion critic, was sitting next to Oscar de la Renta and his entourage, and later wrote that de la Renta repeated "Changed American fashion?" in an incredulous tone.)

The competition for the evening's most prestigious award, Womenswear Designer of the Year, was widely thought to be between de la Renta, who first achieved fame as a society designer in the eighties, and Lang. (The third nominee was Donna Karan.) It was a contest between excess and restraint. When de la Renta won, to wild cheering, it seemed like another sign that the eighties were back in business.

There was a feeling among the people I spoke to after the awards that this time Helmut had gone too far. "We all have to do things we don't want to do sometimes," said Andre Leon Talley, the editor-at-large of *Vogue*. Anna Wintour described Helmut's decision as "a mistake." "If he had been out of the country, maybe, but he was just downtown. I realize he was working," she said, with mock reverence. (Part of the mystique that surrounds Lang derives from the intensity with which he approaches his work, and his Germanic attention to detail. He works "like a wild man," says the artist Jenny Holzer, his friend and sometime collaborator.) Still, Wintour went on, "If I had known he wasn't coming, I would have called him. It was discourteous not to turn up."

Lang has annoyed the American fashion community before by violating the protocol. He has rebelled against the onerous schedule of runway presentations, the four yearly spectacles (two each for the men's and women's lines) at which designers are supposed to submit new work to the scrutiny of the press and of the buyers from the big department stores. Lang shows his men's clothes together with his women's, but even this seems too much for him. (He calls his presentations not collections but seances de travail—working sessions.) A week before his fall-winter, 1998, show, Lang decided to cancel his runway presentation and show pictures of his clothes on the Internet instead. Fashion editors were given CD-roms.

Everyday Clothing as Fashion

Fashion people love to use the word "modern" to justify the latest trend, but the fashion industry is quite unmodern, and becoming steadily more so as its old top-down hierarchy falls farther and farther out of touch with the casual-all-year-long world we live in. The collections are about display, and Helmut Lang has a deep aversion to display. It runs through everything he does, from his minimalism to his conspicuous absence from the American Fashion Awards. This is the way in which Lang really is trying to change the rules—to make fashion less about creating a spectacle for the press and more about the problem most people face when they think of fashion, which is simply what to put on in the morning.

If you go into the Helmut Lang store on Greene Street,

you will see four racks of clothing, two of men's and two of women's. The least expensive clothes in the store, T-shirts and jeans, often hang next to the most expensive items, silk and chiffon dresses and shearling coats. Most designers are careful to keep their high-priced, more formal clothes separate from their lower-priced casual wear. Armani, for example, has an expensive Giorgio Armani line, a sportswear-oriented Emporio Armani line, and a casual A/X Armani Exchange line. Lang has only one line, Helmut Lang, and instead of diversifying as his business grows, he is doing the opposite—his short-lived Helmut Lang Jeans line was recently reabsorbed into the parent.

Lang's mixing of the casual and the formal is not just a matter of marketing; it goes to the core of his aesthetic. His most expensive formal clothes have the ease and simplicity of everyday stuff, and his casual clothes have the correctness and detailing of ready-to-wear. Most high-fashion designers, whose natural leanings are toward ornament and glamour, don't do casual clothes very well—the fabric is too rich, the styling too elaborate. But Lang's distinction as a designer is his instinct for the appeal of the most basic items, like an old blue sweatshirt or a T-shirt worn silky with use, and he has created a whole new genre of luxury casual clothes. According to Katherine Betts, the editor-in-chief of *Harper's Bazaar*, "Lang did for T-shirts and jeans what Ralph Lauren did for club ties and tweed jackets—he made them fashion garments."

This transformation, the making of fashion out of everyday clothes, is a sleight of hand that involves more than just design. It is also a matter of the designer's image: the idea that the brand name conveys. The great couturiers, like Coco Chanel and Christian Dior, stood for the idea of high fashion—an elite enterprise that only the rich could afford. Then came the Italian fashion princes, like Armani and Gianni Versace, who used their own media celebrity to give ready-to-wear clothes the kind of allure that made-to-measure clothes used to have. One cannot see their names without thinking of their faces: fit and bronzed Italian men, relaxing in their villas, attractive in a way that made the clothes attractive. Then came Ralph Lauren, who used "life-style marketing"—associating his clothes with upper-middle-class Americans—to create a new kind of fashion image. Lauren's face was an inescapable part of the image—tanned, smiling, somewhere-out-there-on-the-range Ralph. . . .

The Helmut Lang Style

I met Lang for the first time the day after the American Fashion Awards. Our initial meeting had been cancelled several times, so I expected this appointment to be cancelled, too; Lang, it seems, doesn't divide up his day in an orderly manner, but works intuitively, making of his schedule a raft of different possible commitments and deadlines and ideas, all awaiting the arrival of what he likes to call "the right organic moment." But it appeared that our right organic moment had arrived. . . .

Helmut Lang was dressed in Helmut Lang, too: he was wearing a light-blue button-down shirt with an HL insignia, a crew-neck T-shirt visible underneath; Helmut Lang jeans, the stiff but not lacquered kind; and his new black patent-leather Helmut Lang shoes, without socks. He walked as though he had just dismounted from a motorcycle, legs slightly apart. His dark-brown hair was long and slicked back. When he smiled, his eyes appeared friendlier than his mouth, projecting the simultaneous feeling of ease and reserve you get from his clothes. He looked healthy, even slightly voluptuous, but there was also something "broken" about him, a word once used to describe what he wanted his male models to look like.

It was a blisteringly hot day, but the showroom was cool and white. The fall, 2000, collection was hanging there, and editors and stylists were picking it over for items to use in photo shoots. I admired the gray wool-and-silk suits, which have an emerald shimmer when the silk catches the light. The men's clothes were more flamboyant than the women's. In the nineties, Lang dressed women like men, and earned the love of professional women everywhere. Now, like many other menswear designers, he seems to be trying to dress men like women.

The clothes exhibited certain characteristic Helmut Lang details: a fly-front coat with only one of the buttons exposed, a jean cuffed at a certain place, a strap in the back of a jacket, which is somewhat useful—it lets you hang the coat over your shoulder—but which is also an avant-garde element. At his most radical, he seems to be questioning the basics of what makes clothes clothes. There is a sense of whimsy in Lang. Last year, a padded collar that was clearly derived from those inflatable airplane headrests began showing up on some of the coats, both in the men's and the women's lines. Instead of a designer's personality being grafted onto the clothes through marketing and advertising, there is a personal voice in the clothes, expressed in these odd details and references. . . .

Lang in New York

On a sultry day in August, the usual collection of people was hovering outside the second-floor showroom, all waiting for their right organic moment. Inside, Helmut Lang was supervising a fitting for a friend who was getting married the next day. He wore a tight, mottled gray T-shirt, his usual jeans, no socks, and the patent-leather shoes. The bridegroom and his best man were wearing white suits. Lang looked intently at the pant leg of the groom and instructed one of his assistants to pin it a little higher. The groom's hair was plastered at odd angles. He looked "broken" in the Helmut Lang mode. When Lang finished, he kissed the groom on the cheek and joined me.

I followed him across the street, to look at what will be the new perfumery. The store will eventually have a laboratory, where people will be able to personalize their own scents by blending different oils, and a sales floor above, where items like toothbrushes and soaps will be sold along with the perfumes.

Pointing up Greene Street, Lang explained that his design studio would be moving a block north, to a space above the PaceWildenstein Gallery, later this fall, and that his press office would expand and take over the current building. He is also thinking of opening a made-to-measure store. There were some Con Ed workers up the street, wearing the orange safety vests that Lang made into a motif in several of his late-nineties collections. Once you had seen these vests in the store, you could not look at them without thinking of the orange in a fashion context—not necessarily a good thing. I was wearing a pair of Helmut Lang cargo pants that were several years old. Other designers' clothes often seem dated after a season or two, but not Lang's. In a sense, Helmut Lang has solved the problem of what to wear too well for his own good: when you've got a couple of his uniforms, you don't need to buy any more clothes.

4

EXAMINING POP CULTURE

Fashion, Culture, and Controversy

Symbols as Fashion: Clothing Tie-Symbols

Ruth P. Rubinstein

One of the functions of fashion is identification. For example, teenagers often select the same dress styles worn by their favorite musical performers. Wearing similar clothing creates a bond between teenagers and the musicians. Clothing symbols can indicate that one belongs to a certain group. Members can identify each other. Tie-symbols can also indicate support for causes. For instance, the red ribbons worn in memory of AIDS victims became a tie-symbol when celebrities began sporting them at public events.

In the following article, author Ruth P. Rubinstein, a fashion expert and professor of sociology at the State University of New York at Binghamton, discusses the way clothing tie-symbols are created and perpetrated. This excerpt is from Rubinstein's book, *Dress Codes: Meanings and Messages in American Culture.*

TIE-SYMBOLS ARE EXPRESSIONS OF SUPPORT, OR association, with a particular idea, cause, predicament, or person. For instance, during the Gulf War in January and February 1991, people in the United States took to wearing clothing and accessories emblazoned with the American flag. Wearing the flag was associated with feelings of patriotism and showed support for the men and women in service. Flags

■

could be seen on T-shirts, sweatshirts, swimsuits, beach towels, tote bags, and umbrellas.

A picture of the U.S. Olympic volleyball team printed on the front page of the *New York Times* in summer 1992 showed the teammates with their heads shaven. They shaved their heads as a gesture of solidarity with Bob Samuelson, a team member involved in a dispute with Olympic officials that caused a reversal of the U.S. victory over Japan. Their shaved heads matched his normal "non-do." For them, the shaved head was a tie-symbol; it expressed support for their teammate.

Clothing as Personal Expression

The most visible tie-symbol in 1992–1993 was the inverted red "V" ribbon worn to honor people who have died of acquired immunodeficiency syndrome (AIDS). Since 1991, when the ribbons were designed and worn by a fifteen-member group, Visual AIDS, thousands of the ribbons have been sold. They have become ubiquitous on award shows and on the streets. Their purpose is to display solidarity and sympathy for AIDS victims. A March 1993 report in the *New York Times* pointed out that the AIDS ribbon paved the way for other ribbons—a pink one worn to show breast cancer awareness, and a purple one that calls attention to "the harsh realities of young people growing up in urban neighborhoods."

Tie-symbols are a means of self-association and self-expression, and their adoption is dependent on personal choice. Their term is short and they are ancillary to a person's attire. Concerns, fears, tensions, and hopes within a social aggregate may give rise to tie-symbols. Wearing one announces *sympathy with* a group, a political idea, or a public persona. The tie-symbol can stand for something or against something; it can be pro-social or antisocial. For the wearer, it may or may not have the meaning originally intended.

Advertisers have found that teenagers respond to hero images. These wished-for identities are associated with overcoming obstacles. "Aspirational" has become a marketing buzzword. Aspirational ads are intended to make consumers aspire to, or emulate, the people endorsing the product. Recognizing the benefits of turning clothes into tie-symbols, Levi Strauss hired filmmaker Spike Lee to make the company's commercials. The 1991 ad campaign took viewers to such sites as East Rutherford, New Jersey, where Joe Hamm, a lighting technician, defied heights to prepare the stage for a Grateful Dead concert; New Braunfels, Texas, where spelunkers explored mysterious caves; and Las Vegas, Nevada, where people were making arrangements for a Mike Tyson fight. According to Levi's marketing director, Daniel M. Chew, the Levi spots were intended to make the target audience, the fourteen-to-twenty-four age-group, ask: "Gee, if these guys are doing all this, what could I be doing?" Lee's earlier campaign, "501 Button Fly Report," had been very successful. The ads provided the inspiration for a line of Levi's T-shirts carrying the slogan "Button your fly" and unauthorized versions saying "Unbutton my fly." Both slogans demand action.

Tie-symbols are important in the United States because they provide people with a means of finding out about their own values and goals. In more traditional societies a sense of identity and appropriate goals were handed to the individual by one's religion, family, and community. Such a path is often not easily available in more complex, contemporary societies. Tie-symbols make it possible for a person to play out different roles and try out different values; they also enable individuals to associate themselves with a desired persona, such as Madonna. Tie-symbols make it easier for individuals to find out about different paths and discover ones they might desire; hence, they are popular among the young and with those with less circumscribed lifestyles. Tie-symbols are used by individuals to help *define the self, maintain self-definition,* and *express political values and goals.*

Seeking Self-Definition

The term "reference group" was used by Herbert Hyman in 1942 when he described the phenomenon whereby individuals who do not belong to a particular group (the reference group) use that group's ideas, beliefs, and values to guide their behavior. The reference group provides the standard that is referred to in appropriating an appearance or behavior.

Grade school children are often concerned with *fitting in,* and they prefer wearing what other children in the school wear. They feel a need to dress "like the herd," Elizabeth Hurlock pointed out. They often reject homemade clothing in favor of store-bought clothes. They sometimes resist wearing what their parents want them to wear. Convinced that wearing clothes like those of their classmates will win them acceptance, they explain, "Kids don't want to play with you unless you wear the same clothing they do." Children in the lower grades see the attire chosen by the older students as the preferred style.

Since the 1940s the appearance of adolescents in American society has been remarkably similar to that of their peers and exceptionally different from both adults and younger children. Gaining the *approval of their peers* becomes paramount to youth during their junior and senior high school years, and their attire comes under close peer scrutiny. They realize that they have several choices and that the choices they make can lead to acceptance or rejection by their peers. Their concern with the questions "Who am I?" and "Who do I want to be?" may lead to periodic changes of style.

In the 1990s, spiked hair and pierced ears have been sources of parental anxiety. To gain information that might allay such feelings, Lawrence Kutner interviewed psychiatrists and developmental psychologists specializing in adolescence. The child development experts pointed out that "fashion statements" by adolescents are a part of the road to adulthood; hence, they are a normal phenomenon. Most people adopt the ideals and beliefs of their families when they become adults. The experts recommended that parents allow their children "to make choices and mistakes in this area. Wardrobes can be changed and hair will grow back."

Through the clothing decisions an individual makes, he or she gains greater awareness of a self that is distinct and separate from the family yet still anchored in society's basic ideas and beliefs. The act of wearing peer- or self-designated attire may make it easier to detach oneself from home and family, preparing the individual for the kind of adult independence required in American society.

Adolescent Peer Culture and Trendy Attire

"Schools are not supposed to be a fashion show, yet the halls of high school could pass for runways. For it is in these places of learning—and the streets leading to them—that many fashion trends are born," reported the *New York Times* in 1991. The story noted that the styles of clothing pervasive among rap artists, such as layered hooded sweatshirts, baseball caps, and cable chains with large medallions, have appeared in the collections of Karl Lagarfeld, Charlotte Neuville, and Isaac Mizrahi. Examining attire presently worn in high school may be of help in predicting future fashion.

Examining current styles in high schools in New York, Connecticut, and New Jersey, the reporters for the *New York Times* article found that bagginess was a major trend. Yet although some New York City teenagers insisted on wide-legged, oversized jeans that hang at the waist, sag in the back, and in some cases have two or three inches of cuff, others preferred tight-fitting, straight-legged jeans. In a high school in the Bronx, wearing leggings with long, loose sweaters was considered in style. In Westwood High School in New Jersey, button-down shirts in solid colors with baggy jeans were the representative attire. Students at Greenwich High School in Connecticut liked their jeans tight but torn; in Bridgeport, Connecticut, they liked the preppy look, corduroy and denim. The female students wore shorts and shirts with matching tights.

Bagginess also allows an individual to carry or transport implements of self-protection, such as guns, clubs, or knives; tight-fitting styles do not. High school attire is thus sensitive to specific needs, such as the current concern with safety, and it depends on the cultural and socioeconomic background of the wearer. Students in violence-prone city high schools prefer boots and heavy Bass and Doc Marten's shoes with thick soles to sneakers.

A retrospective study of the clothing experience of students at the Fashion Institute of Technology during adolescence found that many of the students often heard their parents object that "kids go to school to learn, not for a fashion show." Their objections were to no avail, however. Wearing the trendy style enabled the adolescents to "feel at one" with their peers.

Gaining Peer Approval

A strategy used by many adolescents is described in the following quote by one of the Fashion Institute students: "In the beginning of each year from junior to high school, I would look at what everyone else was wearing, then I would simply imitate. . . . I insisted my mother take me shopping each year to remodel my wardrobe. Because if one was seen in last year's fashion, one would be the talk of the town, in a negative way." As another female respondent described the experience: "I can still remember my first pair of designer jeans—Sassoon. Everyone had to have a pair, and everyone who was anyone did. We all looked like clones. But I felt I was a part of a group. It is incredible what a pair of Sassoon jeans could do for one's image. They gave me a sense of security, of being accepted." And another said:

> My best friend had a pair of Nike sneakers, which I wanted very much but [they] were too expensive. Forty dollars was too much at the time. Any kid in school wearing a pair of Nike's was considered "in." I felt "out" because I didn't own a pair. When I finally got the courage to ask Mom to buy me a pair she said "no" and yelled at me for trying to be flashy. I begged and nagged her every day until she couldn't take it anymore. I'll never forget the day she took me to Herman's Sporting Goods Store to purchase my sneakers. I was so happy you couldn't wipe the smile off my face. [But then] in junior high Skippy was the "in" sneaker. All my girlfriends wore them. They were under ten dollars so I bought a few pair. This made my mom real angry, since just the year before she bought me the Nikes, which I stopped wearing. I told her nobody at school wears them anymore, so I couldn't wear them and look stupid. As usual she could not understand why I had to follow what all the other kids wore. . . . I guess parents don't understand peer pressure and the need for kids to feel wanted by a certain group of friends.

That mothers are often cost-conscious and teenagers style-conscious is exemplified in the following story:

> My mother took me and my sister school clothes shopping, which always turned into a nightmare. I wanted the latest fashion and my mother wanted clothes that would last. Buying them a little big so I could wear them the next year also. We often had screaming matches in the stores. Eventually

ucation and a form of fund-raising for environmental cause[s] James Brooks reported in the *New York Times* that T-shirts wer[e] being sold to adults to raise funds for research on how to pro[-]tect sea turtles and were being given free to schoolchildren as [a] means of educating them about the endangered species. . . .

Rejecting the Vietnam War and the draft, hippies adopte[d] an appearance and clothing that reflected their "revolution[?] against rationality, self-restraint, and goal-directed behavio[r,] the values underlying institutional discourse. In contrast to th[e] conformity of the gray flannel suit and the impeccable, mod[-]est mien required by the establishment, they looked dishevele[d] and unkempt. They wore their hair long, and jeans and wor[k] shirts became their "uniform." Young men often wore India[n] headbands, amulets, shell necklaces, beads, and embroidere[d] vests instead of shirts. See-through outfits flaunted sexuality.

The hippies of the 1960s demanded the right to full sel[f-]expression. In a study of hippie communities, D.L. Wiede[r] and D.H. Zimmerman found that immediacy, spontaneity, an[d] hedonism were favored over sobriety and industry. Propert[y] was rejected by the hippies because it identified privilege, an[d] they had no qualms about receiving welfare or panhandling.

As a cohort, a group of people born during the same tim[e] period, this generational unit was critically aware of inequalit[y] and the mindless pursuit of affluence. Rejecting traditiona[l] concepts of career, education, and morality, they produced [a] culture in opposition to technocracy. They searched for alter[-]natives to the prevalent traditions of lifestyle and occupation[-]ally linked identity. Their disaffiliation took different forms[.] For some it was militant and political; for others it was mysti[-]cal and religious.

my father had to take me, which was great because he let me get what I wanted and would spend more.

Negative Aspects

Some teenagers whose parents cannot or will not buy them the "right" clothes steal, mug, and even murder to get such clothes. Most, however, go to work. A young man whose family had immigrated from Taiwan when he was eight years old described his experience in this manner:

> In junior high school I became brand conscious. I started working on the weekend delivering Chinese food [and] earning $200 to $250. This was disposable income. Everything I bought was "brand-labeled." Nike and Puma sneakers. Calvin Klein and Sassoon and Sergio Valente jeans. Members Only jackets. I almost had everything I wanted. During my high school days Japanese fashion became "in" [1982–1983]. The clothing [sic] were layered and loose fitting. They were not cheap. A jacket was $350 to $450 and sweaters $100 to $150. They were not boring and made me feel great. Now I was an American. I belonged.

The desire for peer approval has often incorporated a concern with weight. "The height of the disco period was in my ninth grade [1979]," reported a female student. The movies *Thank God It's Friday* and *Saturday Night Fever* were very popular. As she described it:

> The common dress for girls my age were [sic] Danskin bodysuit worn with designer jeans. We competed with one another to lose weight. I was very successful at losing ten pounds and decided to keep on dieting. My anorexia craze ended once I reached a hundred pounds. My menstrual period stopped for six months and was extremely painful when it resumed. I learned my lesson the hard way.

Celebrity Influences

At Brooklyn Technical High School, across the street from Spike's Place, Spike Lee's retail shop, many students wear baseball caps with the letter "X," a promotional item for the director's movie on Malcolm X. Some students at Brooklyn

Tech and other schools say they wear the hats, Malcolm X buttons, and other accessories because they support the slain leader's more aggressive approach to black civil rights.

Becoming popular among them in the summer of 1992 was the bandanna handkerchief tied on the head in an urban-gypsy style. It was folded into a triangle, pulled back over the skull, and knotted in back, as Woody Hochswender reported in the *New York Times*. He noted that John McEnroe wore a pink paisley bandanna for the U.S. Open and "was savagely chic." Photographer Bruce Weber was well known for the practice and not just for hacking around in the garden: "He went hanky-on-top to [*Vogue* editor] Anna Wintour's little soiree at the Paramount Hotel last week." Weber gave legitimacy to the look by wearing it to Anna Wintour's party.

For teens of the 1980s the movie *Flashdance* and MTV were important sources of style. Referring to *Flashdance*, one said, "I remember going home and cutting up all my sweatshirts." Another noted, "My mom thought I was crazy cutting up perfectly good shirts and turning them into rags." And another related, "The movie had a big impact on us kids who watched it. Even guys wore cut shirts and sweatshirts that bared their shoulders and belly buttons." A ripped sweatshirt became the desired style.

With the start of MTV in 1981, music and fashion began to go hand in hand for the younger teenage group. Madonna's style had a significant impact. Prior to 1983 and Madonna's impact, the oversized man-tailored shirt and tight jeans were the most visible trend for this age-group. Only a few other trends were seen, such as the short dresses, usually in black, of teens in the Punk movement in the East Village in New York. Madonna's videos *Borderline*, *Lucky Star*, and *Like a Virgin* showed her first "look": a short black dress, big cross earrings, silver and rubber bracelets, black crosses and many silver chains worn around the neck, and a bare midriff. The short tube skirt, tank tops, cropped leggings, and fingerless gloves that Madonna wore became "required attire" among the younger teenage set. Fashion forecasters predicted these elements would be the rage for girls up to sixteen. Hundreds of young girls showed up at Macy's in New York for a "Desperately Madonna Contest," a look-alike contest held after the

movie *Desperately Seeking Susan*. As one responder [ ]t: "I loved the way Madonna dressed—and I dre [ ]ace outfits, spandex leggings, tight miniskirts, and t [ ]ber bracelets.". . .

Maintaining Self-Definition

The Yale School of Drama is "filled with sufferin[ ] dressed in black," reported Alex Witchel in a 1991 artic[ ] *New York Times Magazine*. Entering college freshmen [ ] particular type of sneaker, jacket, or color in vogue in a [ ]ar school. It reaffirms and maintains their new associati[ ]

A 1982 study by Margaret Rucker and her colleag[ ] the University of California, Davis, provided informati[ ] how the problem of self-definition is worked out in c[ ] The researchers found that students in different n[ ] tended to wear different styles: A long ethnic dress iden[ ] female students majoring in art; a suit (blouse, skirt,[ ] jacket) characterized textile and clothing students; jeans[ ] plaid shirts were the choice of engineering and psychol[ ] majors; overalls were worn by those studying animal scier[ ] Students adopt the appropriate styles to show they are c[ ] nected to a particular social aggregate. They thus announ[ ] that they have a particular identity and a social base within t[ ] larger university population. Here, reference group attire ac[ ] to *deindividuate*. It helps to create a social entity within a con[ ] text of ongoing interaction. . . .

Expressing Political Values and Goals

Groups and aggregates desiring, protesting, or rejecting a political agenda may signify their sentiments in their dress. In the United States such expressions vary. They may involve (1) identifying the side one is on, (2) taking a stand and dressing the part, and, sometimes, (3) hiding one's identity.

The most familiar, popular, and least tumultuous example of political attire is the slogan T-shirt, which came into being in the 1960s. Many artists were involved in such projects, the best known being British designer Katharine Hamnett. She received so many requests for her T-shirts that she had to stop making them in 1987.

In 1991 T-shirts were used as a means of environmental ed-

Patriotism and Fashion During the Spanish-American War

Rob Schorman

On February 2, 1898, the U.S. battleship *Maine* was attacked off the coast of Cuba. The *Maine* sank, resulting in 260 fatalities. While it was unclear who was responsible for the attack, Americans suspected Spanish saboteurs, and the incident would become known as the attack that started the Spanish-American War.

Americans responded with a rise in patriotism, a response that inspired the fashion industry in several ways. New styles incorporated designs such as eagles and flags, while storeowners capitalized on the patriotic mood by including pro-American themes in their advertisements and window displays. Not everyone supported this display of patriotism, however; some Americans called the "commercialization of war" inappropriate, arguing that it was disrespectful to use flag imagery to sell merchandise. Author Rob Schorman examines how Americans during wartime expressed their patriotism through the clothes they wore. Schorman is an assistant professor of history at Miami University in Ohio.

IN THE LATE 1890S, AMERICANS OFTEN CONfronted the relationship between citizenship and clothing. On

■

the city streets immigrants wore new clothes as a self-conscious assertion of their Americanization. In newspapers, magazines, and store windows, advertisers sold everything from men's suits to women's corsets by associating them with events such as the election of President McKinley, George Washington's birthday, and the Declaration of Independence. During the Spanish-American War of 1898, as American nationalistic fervor reached new heights, so did its linkage with dress. Military braid and buttons appeared as fashion details on dresses, capes, and hats. The *New York Journal* published a full page of testimonials urging a boycott of Parisian fashions because of France's supposed sympathy with Spain. Even schoolchildren made the connection. Ethel Spencer, who grew up near Pittsburgh and would have been eight or nine years old at the time, recalled the era in her memoirs:

> The Spanish dress too had a long, but dishonorable career. It was made for me while the Spanish war was in progress— a red and yellow gingham, the colors of Spain. How my patriotic soul hated that dress! My schoolmates teased me every time I wore it, called me Spanish, implied I was a traitor; but I had to wear it anyway. And when I thankfully outgrew it, it passed to Mary and then to Elizabeth carrying with it a heavy load of built-in hatred. I don't think my little sisters had the faintest idea why it was hateful, but they loyally hated it anyway.

The sinking of the U.S. battleship *Maine* in Havana harbor on 2 February 1898 with the loss of nearly 260 men provided a focus and rallying cry for pro-war agitation. Though subsequent investigations failed to prove Spanish complicity, many Americans blamed the explosion that destroyed the *Maine* on Spanish saboteurs. During the public outcry that followed, one Boston clothing store labeled all the price cards in its front window with the slogan, "Remember the *Maine*, boys, and the price of this suit.". . .

The "war fever" that gripped the United States in 1898 had been building since 1895, when Cuban revolutionaries mounted an armed insurrection against Spanish colonial rule. The rebels actively cultivated U.S. sympathy and found fertile ground in doing so. For many Americans, the United States' own heritage of revolt against a European ruler created an affinity for the Cuban nationalists and a complementary distaste for seeing a colonial state wield power so close to U.S. shores. The Spanish did not help their cause by pursuing harshly repressive countermeasures in Cuba and adopting an arrogant and occasionally openly dismissive attitude toward U.S. diplomatic interest in the conflict. American newspapers fanned sympathies with melodramatic and spectacular accounts of events connected to the insurrection. Sensing the popular appeal of the issue, politicians seized upon the Cuban cause as a campaign issue, further heightening the rhetoric and emotions surrounding the events. Overwhelming public support continued as the United States mobilized for a conflict that ended in the summer of 1898 with a decisive defeat of Spain and the establishment of the United States as an imperial power. . . .

The 1890s had been especially trying for Americans. Labor conflicts such as the Homestead and Pullman strikes in 1892 and 1894 produced what historian Alan Trachtenberg has called "the most destructive civil violence since the Civil War." A serious economic depression battered the country from 1893 to 1897, and the 1896 presidential election between William Jennings Bryan and William McKinley was starkly divisive. Although the U.S. population grew more closely linked through its expanding economic, communications, and transportation systems, the country remained divided by sectional differences and a growing demographic diversity as waves of immigrants from eastern and southern Europe poured into America. Sectionalism and ethnic differences threatened the Victorian American view of a settled world order and posed a new challenge to a concept of "Americanness" that had rested comfortably on Anglo-Protestant middle-class values. The Spanish-American War helped mask this divisiveness in a new spirit of national pride. Economically, politically, ideologically, and emotionally, the war made sense to a great many Americans.

Advertising the War

But patriotism and citizenship are abstract concepts that require symbolic expression to become part of public culture.

Certainly the vivid illustrations and headlines of the new mass media provided something of this sort. So did a revived "cult of the flag" that emerged in the late nineteenth century and raised veneration for the Stars and Stripes as a national emblem to a new level. National identity also infiltrated everyday life in less overt but more pervasive ways through the objects of daily existence, including clothing. . . .

Clothing manufacturers and retailers were quick to seize on the opportunity to link their products to nationalistic fervor. In early March 1898, the *Chicago Dry Goods Reporter* published a column describing how to make an effective window display based on the sinking of the *Maine:* "The window dresser who is ever alert for novelty will not allow the disaster to the battleship *Maine* to pass without getting an idea out of it for a window display." The feature offered tips for a display involving a bust swaddled in flowing white fabric to represent Columbia—"white cashmere is the best goods to use for this drapery." The writer further suggested using red, white, and blue bunting, an American flag, a pair of crossed oars, a wreath labeled "In Memory of the *Maine* Heroes," perhaps pictures of the *Maine* or its crew, and, of course, the goods. "This idea would work well with a display of wash dress goods," the writer added, "but it would also look well with black goods or others lines."

In many advertisements, clothing merchants pushed the link between war news and store news, sometimes with only passing reference in an illustration or headline but other times more extensively. Wanamaker's in New York City ran an advertisement showing a fashionably dressed woman standing at attention and delivering a salute, although the text made no reference to the military conflict. Saks in Indianapolis ran an advertisement that proclaimed, "We stand by our colors," again without overt reference to the war, followed by a generic testimony to the reliability of its goods. Some references were more specific, if no less strained, as in headlines such as "Manila has fallen and so have our prices" or "We would like to C-U-B-A purchaser of a pair of our stylish fitting shoes."

Other advertisers devoted their entire space to the war theme. W.C. Loftus, a New York tailor, ran an ad that boasted, "Into the enemy's ranks goes the hot shot from our guns. . . .

The suits that we make to order for $15.00 are the amunition [*sic*] with which we are reducing the ranks of the higher priced tailors." An Indianapolis shoe merchant, using rhyming text with a specially commissioned illustration, linked his merchandise to the war effort under the headline "Uncle Sam . . . Crushing a Tarantula." The text read:

> One foot is placed upon the Don—
> (The other foot's in Washington)—
> Both feet are dressed in honest leather
> To stand all kinds of wear and weather.
> In short, our Uncle Sam had got
> Shoes just like those sold by Marott.

The effort to stay in step with the news was evident. Readers could find on one page of a Chicago newspaper a story headlined "President's Call for 75,000 More Volunteers"; on the opposite page of the same edition an ad proclaimed: "Uncle Sam means business and wants 75,000 more fighters. The style and quality of Foreman's Challenge Shoes prove that we mean business and we are doing it too."

The Hub, a Chicago department store, ran a weekly advertisement depicting a battle scene accompanied by a headline and introduction tied closely to the latest war news. In mid-June, naval officer Richmond Hobson undertook a daring mission in the harbor of Santiago de Cuba, attempting to trap the Spanish fleet by scuttling a small ship right under the noses of enemy cannons in the harbor entrance. Within a week, The Hub ran an advertisement with a custom-made illustration and text reading: "It was Hobson's choice to risk his life in the fiery mouth of Santiago. . . . For eleven years The Hub—through choice—has braved the storms of competition."

Later that month, General William Shafter, field commander of the U.S. ground forces during the war, sent his troops ashore in Cuba. Within days The Hub illustrated the event in an ad that opened: "Shafter holds the key to the gates of Cuban liberty and The Hub holds the key to the clothing trade of Chicago." The advertising manager for this store once told an interviewer that he always tried to base his advertisements on current events: "The public eye, you know, is always focused upon some particular thought or event. It is my aim to always be within that focus and the nearer the center the better."

Some of these advertising tactics amounted to nothing more than the graphic art of self-defense. As news articles became more dramatic and sensational, advertisers raised the volume of their appeals to avoid getting drowned out. Some of the marketing methods were just business as usual; advertisers employed war motifs just as they had used the Klondike gold

Being a Patriot Comes Back into Fashion

Since the [terrorist attack on America on] Sept. 11, 2001, the term "buying American" has new meaning. Flag-logo clothing from Tommy and Ralph has come back out of the closet. Patriotic ribbons have sprouted on lapels. A new sense of pride in Old Glory, and the fact that in many cases, purchasing anything red, white and blue means green for relief efforts, is inspiring a buying frenzy of star-spangled clothing and accessories.

"Normally, people want flag fashions for Fourth of July celebrations or political conventions," says Maureen Bailey, one of the owners of patrioticjewelry.com, a website specializing in Americana-themed costume jewelry. "Now we can't keep things like our $15 flag pin in stock. We've gotten so many hits the website has crashed four times." Some retailers have been overwhelmed by the demand for anything American-themed. Old Navy, which sold $5 flag-emblazoned Fourth of July T-shirts earlier this summer, put its remaining stock online at www.oldnavy.com, then scrambled to release a new limited-quantity special-edition T-shirt, featuring just Old Glory (no Old Navy logo) and the words "United States of America."

"The shirts hit 300 stores across the country," says Jessica O'Callaghan, Old Navy spokesperson. "All proceeds of the special-edition T-shirts, which sell for $5, will benefit the New York Community Trust's Sept. 11 Fund."

Sears is selling men's, women's and children's screen-

rush, the election of 1896, the latest stage sensation, or any other current event as grist for the ad copywriters' mill. In part, the merchandising strategies were a testament to mass-market capitalism's capacity to take virtually any human activity or aspiration and turn it into a sales opportunity.

But trends in advertising connote more than mere sales pitches; advertising, like clothing, helps define certain basic

print patriotic T-shirts in its 860 department stores. With such slogans as "God Bless America" and "United We Stand," the shirts sell for $10 or less. The chain is donating 50 percent of sales to the American Red Cross and its emergency relief efforts. At Target, consumers can find red, white and blue T-shirts for the entire family. Designs, which include flags, stars and stripes and other patriotic themes, retail for $4 to $5 depending on size. Claire's, an accessory store, has red, white and blue glitter tattoos, belts and bangles.

Tiffany has received orders for a $60,000 flag pin from customers who wanted the antique piece featured in the jeweler's ad after the tragedy. Monet is making a $15 jeweled flag pin for Lord & Taylor to help fund a disaster relief charity. Connecticut jewelry and accessories designer Carolee will be donating all of the proceeds from the sales of her three American flag pins to the American Red Cross. The pins, which range in price from $20 to $50, are available at www.carolee.com and in better specialty and department stores.

Nordstrom spokeswoman Danielle Deabler says the store's Swarovski crystal American flag pin, $98, sold out in a matter of days. . . .

"Used to be that people might wear a flag shirt or pin to a picnic or parade. Now customers are looking for a way to show their support and patriotism," says Deabler. "When life changes, fashion changes with it."

Korky Vann, "Being a Patriot Comes Back into Fashion," *Hartford Courant*, October 4, 2001.

categories of social knowledge and terms of public discourse. These "coordinates of meaning" become common frames of reference that move beyond the purely commercial realm. In response to criticism over desecration of the flag, *Printers' Ink*, an advertising trade journal, responded: "The flag has never been more widely used for advertising purposes than it is to-day; yet never has it evoked more enthusiasm and patriotic ardor." However self-serving, this statement is essentially true: Advertisers perpetuate and legitimate values even as they attempt to appropriate them.

While advertisers in other fields also adopted war motifs, the relationship was especially powerful for clothiers and dry goods merchants. While Americans did not furnish their houses with Army cots or alter their diets to simulate military rations, they did adorn themselves with emblems of patriotism and adapt military motifs to a variety of garment designs. Thus, clothing ads evoked not only a nationalistic discourse of advertising but a nationalistic discourse of fashion as well. As a result, the merger of merchandising strategies and nationalistic zeal seemed to know no bounds among clothing and dry goods merchants in 1898. A single 1898 issue of the *Dry Goods Economist*, a trade journal, contained 82 advertisements with war themes. War relics—captured flags, battle swords, and so forth—became hot items in window displays, and traffic in them became so lively that trade publications warned merchants against counterfeiters.

The effort went beyond advertisements and window displays to store decorations and special promotions, even to the type of merchandise sold. One writer suggested that a successful "fall fashion opening" could be arranged around an "Army camp" theme. Customers invited to the store would be offered some facsimile of hardtack as refreshments and receive military-style buttons as souvenirs. "And if you could get several of the soldier boys lately returned home to act as ushers, in uniform," the writer concluded, "of course, it would make a big hit."

Wartime Trends in Fashion

Large department stores enticed shoppers with popular tableaux vivant, in which mannequins or actors depicted war celebrities in various poses. As successful battle reports began to come in, wholesalers rushed into the marketplace with patriotic souvenirs such as lapel pins, buttons, buckles, badges, toys, puzzles, and knickknacks. Merchants were advised to add these items to their product lines or simply to purchase a quantity as promotional items. Taking advantage of the celebrity of war hero Admiral George Dewey, one St. Louis department store advertised, "Dewey souvenir bargains in every department, in every aisle, on every counter." The *Dry Goods Economist* observed that "the whole market seems to be rampant with patriotism" and later asked, in its "Wide-Awake Retailing" column: "Are you reaping the harvest that the wave of patriotism is bringing to every live dry goods man?"

Consumers for the most part accepted the mix of consumption and patriotism, buying red, white, and blue ribbons, neckwear, fans, hatbands, parasols, vest chains, walking canes—even garters and petticoats. They purchased suspenders with portraits of Admiral Dewey or images of the battleship *Maine* woven into the design; they wore belt buckles ornamented with eagles, swords, and flags. They bought veils with "all styles of red, white and blue chenille dots and borders"; tri-color shirtwaists and straw hats; handkerchiefs in red, white, and blue; and handkerchiefs with Dewey's portrait or depictions of the American and Cuban flags. They wore badges and emblems shaped like military decorations; they favored faux military buttons on belts, cufflinks, studs, and hat pins; they used lace pins topped with tiny knapsacks and flags—in short, war motifs appeared on nearly every type of personal clothing or object.

Fashion cut and detail were also affected, as garments began to appear trimmed a la militaire. An advertisement in the *Ladies' Home Journal* declared that military-style capes were "a necessary article in the wardrobe of patriotic American women," and fashion columnists recommended adding a military collar decorated with fiat gold braid and brass stars to bring the previous year's outerwear and dresses up to date. Cavalry caps were popular as casual headwear for both women and children. Bunting, the worsted material used to make flags, gained favor as dress material. Popular colors included army gray, army blue, and army red, as well as navy blue, artillery red, cadet gray, battle gray, and later "Sampson blue" and "rough rider brown," after Admiral William Sampson and Theodore Roosevelt's famous volunteer regiment, respectively. In the meantime, yellow became distinctly unfashionable because of its association with the color of the Spanish flag. The "Spanish flounce," a popular design treatment early in the year, was reborn as the "Dewey flounce." Fashion writers also promoted "Dewey vests, Dewey hats," and "Roosevelt cloth."

Critics and Boycotts

Some manufacturers and retailers initially were dubious about war fever. In February 1898, the *Chicago Dry Goods Reporter*, fearing the effect the war might have on business, editorialized against "the tendency among the more irresponsible jingo dailies to shout for war." Soon, however, the popular journals and trade publications climbed aboard without qualification and encouraged support for the war in clothing and personal items. "Even the most conservative women [are] yielding to this patriotic fancy," the Designer announced, and the *Chicago Dry Goods Reporter* assured its readers: "The American woman's dress may bear the stamp of patriotism in elegance and proclaim her pride of country effectively and unobtrusively, with no sacrifice of modesty and good taste."

The proposed boycott of Paris clothing received widespread publicity. "American women now have as good an opportunity to prove their patriotism as the men who shoulder muskets and go to the front," said Harriet Pullman, widow of railcar tycoon George Pullman. "A true American woman will make any sacrifice for her country's dignity, and is willing to wear homespun if necessary." The *New York Journal* published a compendium of dispatches from Philadelphia, St. Louis, Cincinnati, Boston, Charleston, and Savannah indicating the boycott was spreading across the country. The *Indianapolis News* ran headlines such as "Patriotic Women. They will Not Buy Anything that is Manufactured in France" and the *Chicago Tribune* urged that "the leading society women all over the country join . . . in inducing their friends to buy only homemade styles or those which come from London."

It is difficult to know how significant this effort might have become because the war lasted only from April until August. By the time the fall and winter styles came on the market and the nation's fashion resolve might have been truly tested, the fighting was over. Some of the stylistic innovations lingered, however. Just as certain men dramatized "strenuous life" masculinity during the war and continued to act on this philosophy in daily life during the years immediately succeeding it, so men's fashion for the next several years continued to offer clothing with military motifs such as a "military sack suit" or "army shoulders." In 1903 a women's tailoring journal commented on the popularity of certain "military effects" in female fashion, describing them as "decorative details of feminine warpaint."

Not everyone accepted commercialization of the war effort. The *American Banner* of Philadelphia attacked "imbecile advertisers" who capitalized on war news in their publicity. Fashion and advertising using the American flag aroused particular controversy: "'Do I think it shows true respect to our flag to see it made up into gowns, fashioned into shirt waists, turned into petticoats and utilized for stockings?' repeated a Brooklyn woman yesterday. . . . 'Most assuredly I do not.'" Others, however, responded, "I do not think we can ever see that flag too often. No matter where it appears, it is an evidence of patriotism." Further, "I cannot think it possible for women to show real disregard for the significance of the flag, or that any irreverence can be meant by the most excessive display of the colors, and even in an apparently exaggerated way of personal adornment.". . .

Clothing and Nationalism

The popular zeal for the Spanish-American War offered the opportunity to rally around the flag both literally and symbolically. According to historian John Bodnar, "As American society simultaneously became more integrated economically and more diverse culturally, an attempt was made to fashion patriotic symbols that would appeal to the broadest possible segment of the nation." Although Bodnar was referring specifically to the flag, clothing styles disseminated by the new mass media accomplished a similar function in ways that, being less direct, may have been all the more effective. Americans pieced together their own senses of nationalism and made their own claims to "proper" citizenship in no small part through their manipulation of the material goods at their disposal. . . .

Symbols in the United States have had a special significance because the nation was founded with a break from the past and an influx of new residents, and its national symbols have had to be invented and accessible. According to historian and political theorist Michael Walzer, "American symbols and ceremonies are culturally anonymous, invented rather than inherited, voluntaristic in style, narrowly political in content." Such symbols were all the more important in the 1890s because the diversity and newness of U.S. society meant that it couldn't claim primordial ties of tradition, ethnic heritage, or religion. All nationalities are essentially constructed, but the newness of the United States means the invented aspects of its nationalism lie closer to the surface than in many other countries. In addition, the U.S. Constitution failed to define citizenship or describe exactly how it was to be obtained. As Walzer wrote, "The Flag and the Pledge are, as it were, all we have."

Frumpy or Chic: Professors' Dress Styles and Their Campus Image

Alison Schneider

Trends in college fashion are often associated with students. As author Alison Schneider reveals, however, professors are also subject to clothing crises and stereotypes. Schneider looks at the expectations held by students and other faculty regarding professors' dress styles. She describes the association between "frumpy" clothing and intelligence. Traditionally, academics are often thought to be too busy with scholarly concerns to worry about their appearance. Well-dressed faculty, by comparison, are thought to be less serious than their more casually attired counterparts—a perception that may affect one's job status, or even getting hired in the first place.

Schneider also discusses how some professors use fashion to explore—and repress—gender and ethnic identity. While universities have become more tolerant regarding personal expression in the classroom, ethnic dress, youthful styles, and other nontraditional fashions remain controversial choices. The pressure to wear serious clothing is even greater for women, who are still held to stricter standards than men. Alison Schneider is a contributing writer for the *Chronicle of Higher Education*.

■

THERE WAS JUST ONE PROBLEM WITH THE EN-glish department's job candidate: his pants.

They were polyester, green polyester, and the members of the hiring committee considered that a serious offense. For 10 minutes they ranted about the cut, the color, the cloth. Then and only then did they move on to weightier matters.

He did not get the job. Neither did a woman lugging an oversized tote bag (too working-class). Or a man sporting a jaunty sweater and scarf (too flaky). Or a woman in a red-taffeta dress and cowboy boots (too—well, too much).

In the world of academe, where the life of the mind pre-vails, does it really matter if a scholar wears Gucci, gabardine, or grunge? What about good looks? Can such things tip the scales in a job interview, weaken a bid for tenure, or keep you off the A list on the conference circuit? Many professors say they can, although there is quibbling over the reasons why.

Intellect Versus Fashion

Talk about appearances might seem unjustified given the pro-fession's showing in the arena of good looks and good taste. "Academics are still the worst-dressed middle-class occupa-tional group in America," says Valerie Steele, chief curator at the museum of the Fashion Institute of Technology and editor of *Fashion Theory: The Journal of Body, Dress & Culture*.

But despite their threadbare reputation, scholars spend a lot of time thinking, talking, and writing about appearances. Last month, Elaine Showalter, an English professor at Prince-ton University, came out of the closet, so to speak, and admit-ted in *Vogue* magazine that she has a fetish for fashion. She waxed eloquent about her Cossack minidress and turquoise boots from Bologna. "For years," she wrote, "I've been trying to make the life of the mind coexist with the day at the mall."

She is not alone. Scholars squirm when the topic of ap-pearance arises, but a growing number agree that even in the ivory tower, image and intellect are hopelessly intertwined.

"I absolutely judge what people wear," says Wayne Koesten-baum, an English professor at the City University of New York's Graduate School and University Center, who dabs on specific perfumes to pay homage to particular writers. (He de-clined to provide an example. "It's much too personal," he says.)

But "there are people who are as excited as I am by certain ideas, certain artistic movements. There are semiotic codes of dress, makeup, and hair that say things about your allegiances."

He should know. He dyed his hair red when he entered graduate school. "It was intimately connected to my intellectual advancement and my movement into feminist and gay theory."

That sounds like self-conscious gobbledygook to some professors. When it comes to appearances, academe breaks down into two camps: pro-frumpy and pro-fashion. Fans of frumpiness insist that if you want to prove you're intellectually a cut above the competition, think twice before parading around in an Italian-cut blazer.

"If it's a choice between being chic or frumpy, I think it benefits academics more to be frumpy," says Emily Toth, a professor of English and women's studies at Louisiana State University. "If you look like you spend too much time on your clothes, there are people who will assume that you haven't put enough energy into your mind." Dr. Toth, who doubles in her off-hours as Ms. Mentor—the Miss Manners of academe—has dished out pithy advice for years, first in a column for *Concerns*, the journal of the Women's Caucus of the Modern Language Association, and now in a book, *Ms. Mentor's Impeccable Advice for Women in Academia.*

Dressing for the Classroom

As for the taffeta dress and cowboy boots—which Ms. Mentor saw for herself—such an outfit may signal that a scholar doesn't grasp the right professional priorities, she says in an interview. "If you don't know how to dress, then what else don't you know? Do you know how to advise students or grade papers? The clothes are part of the judgment of the mind."

Clothes also help determine if someone will fit into a particular institution. Ask around, and you'll hear professors talk about regional norms for academics: The Midwest dresses down, the South dresses up. Tailored but casual wins the day in the Northeast, and anything goes in California—as long as it looks good. Not to mention the fact that individual universities have their own idiosyncratic norms, which professors ignore at their peril.

"A lot depends on institutional context," explains Catharine

R. Stimpson, dean of the graduate school of arts and sciences at New York University. "At a small, fraught department, where everybody is out to get everybody else, they'd use anything—they could even use a little Liz Claiborne—as a sign of overreaching."

Perhaps the biggest liability of looking too good is that colleagues and students may spend more time thinking about what a professor wears than what he or she says. When clothes become a distraction, the frumpiness faction contends, they do a disservice to young scholars who are trying to establish themselves in their field.

Men occasionally take flak for putting too much of a premium on their own appearance. People still talk about what Andrew Ross, the ultra-hip director of the American-studies program at N.Y.U., wore to the M.L.A.'s 1991 meeting: a yellow Comme des Garçons blazer, a Japanese hand-painted tie, and wedge-heeled suede shoes. Back then, Mr. Ross told the *New York Times* that the jacket was "a sendup of the academic male convention of yellow polyester," but these days he doesn't care to comment. Little wonder. The outfit made him a legend in some eyes and a laughingstock in others.

Still, he says, "I don't think it's a bad thing that academics think more about their appearance right now, when the profession is under siege. It translates into a perception that they're not otherworldly, that they don't live in ivory towers, that they meet people where they are rather than tell them where they ought to be." His only fashion regret: removing his earrings when he went on the market. It didn't even land him a job.

"Dressing fashionably in academia is like clearing the four-foot high jump. The bar is not that high," says Michael Berube, an English professor at the University of Illinois at Urbana-Champaign. "Anything with some cut or color draws derision—and admiration—because the sartorial requirements of the business are so low."

Mr. Berube may know whereof he speaks. He showed up at last month's M.L.A. meeting sporting an electric-blue suit of 100-per-cent polyester. He loves the outfit: "It's an amazing color, and it never loses its crease!"

A man may be able to pull off an electric-blue suit without raising eyebrows, but what about a woman? "I still think there's a predisposition to take men more seriously," says Donna C. Stanton, a professor of French and women's studies at the University of Michigan. Junior-faculty women face a particularly difficult quandary, she says. "How do they convey professional seriousness without looking like a man in drag?"

Here's the short list of Ms. Mentor's do's and don'ts: For starters, younger women should play down their sexuality. Skirts should be knee-length or below. Pants are never appropriate for interviews. Steer clear of high-heeled shoes. Choose dark colors over light ones. Ms. Mentor recommends dark purple: "It looks good on everyone."

Teaching Is a Performance Art

But some people think playing by the rules is the riskiest move of all. "I don't think frumpy gets you anywhere except forgotten," says Jane Gallop, a professor of English and comparative literature at the University of Wisconsin at Milwaukee. She's made strong fashion statements for years. She wore velvet jeans and a sweater when she went on the job market; donned a now-legendary skirt made of men's ties when she lectured on psychoanalytic theory and the phallus; and slipped into suede fringed pants and cowboy boots to talk about Western civilization.

She hasn't toned down her look much since her junior-professor days. "I teach in torn T-shirts that I have actually torn myself," she says. And she still defends using clothing as conceptual art: "There's a stupid impression that a lack of style signifies seriousness, but anyone who comes from a literary sense of things knows that style is often the best way to convey complicated things. You should use everything you have to make people think."

Dr. Showalter agrees: "Teaching is performance. We use everything we've got, and costume is part of it. That's not to say that you dress up like Emma Bovary, but a little liveliness is desirable."

"Give me a break," replies Camille Paglia, a humanities professor at the University of the Arts. "Yes, teaching is a performance art. But when the teacher hijacks the classroom for self-display—of fashion or mannerism or cult of personality—we have a corruption of education. Professors think, 'They're here because of me, because of my wonderful whimsy, my wonderful way of doing things.' It makes me want to throw up." Ms. Paglia favors pantsuits for public lectures—she's especially fond of her flowing, Donna Karan tuxedo suit—but sticks to simple slacks, a plain jacket, and rubber-soled shoes in the classroom.

What does all this sartorial sniping mean for scholars going on the job market and the people who are grooming them? Professors spend an inordinate amount of time fine-tuning not only what their protégés will say at interviews but also how they will look when they say it. Mentors criticize everything from the studs in the job-seekers' ears to the shoes on their feet.

The result: Scholars hunting for jobs are expected to look far better than those who have one, says Nancy K. Miller, an English professor at CUNY's graduate school. "I wonder if the emphasis on appearance at the hiring level isn't a displacement of the real issue: that these students aren't going to get jobs. We focus on their clothing as if the perfect suit or haircut, or the toning down of extravagant styles, will guarantee them a job." Alas, she says, it won't.

Ethnic Garb

The deconstruction of dress weighs particularly heavily upon minority professors. "There is a special turn of the knife for racial and ethnic women," says Nell Painter, a black historian at Princeton. "There are prejudices against people who look too Jewish, too working-class, too Italian, too black, or too much of anything different." She adds, however, that "if you look too WASPish, that's probably all right."

The stakes are high for blacks, Ms. Painter says, because nothing they do is neutral. "If you wear a pair of classic trousers and no kente cloth, that makes a statement. And if you wear kente cloth, that makes a statement."

"My difficulty with that," says Karla F.C. Holloway, director of African and African-American studies at Duke University, "is that it makes the other parts of you invisible—your scholarship, your intellect, your seriousness." That's why she favors formality. She doesn't repress her African-American roots—she wears ethnic prints and wraps her hair in a braid, like her grandmother did—but she steers clear of casual couture. "Casualness has never been part of our professional de-meanor," she says. "Maybe because we can't afford to make it part of our professional demeanor."

The most glaring exception may be Robin D.G. Kelley, a historian at N.Y.U. He does have some designer suits in his closet, but most days he pulls on a pair of black jeans, black combat boots, and a "contemporary"—meaning '50s-looking—shirt or sweater.

Students think he's hip and approachable. But looking cool has its cost. "At every stage in my career, youth and informality—in dress, in appearance, in presentation—have been the bane of my existence. Professors take me less seriously."

Fortunately, Dr. Kelley says he has found that "the one thing that speaks louder than dress is the work that you do."

Hair, however, is something else entirely. "People lose their jobs over how they style their hair," he says. A big Afro is associated with late-'60s radicalism, while straightened hair signals that you're a "serious sell-out white wannabe." Braids, dreadlocks, and shaved heads give the impression that you've got a chip on your shoulder. "When I had my hair short, I was a safe Negro," Dr. Kelley says. Now he's growing dreadlocks, a decision that's cramping his style when it comes to his current work, a book about Thelonious Monk. He'd like to don the kind of funky hats that the jazz pianist wore, but he can't until his hair finishes "locking," he says. "It's really messing up my vibe."

Good Looks Can Be Problematic

Things are complicated in other ways for those professors—men or women, white or black—graced with exceptionally good looks. In academe, beauty is a double-edged sword. Scholars, like everybody else, sometimes assume that a sound mind isn't likely to be accompanied by a sexy body.

Bennett Link, a physicist at Montana State University at Bozeman, posed bare-chested last year in the "Studmuffins of Science" calendar, a tongue-in-cheek tribute to good-looking geeks. The attention over his appearance as "Dr. April" has died down, but he admits that when the calendar came out, he wanted to keep it quiet.

"The way a person looks doesn't play much of a role in the

sciences," he says. In fact, he adds, it's a matter of pride among scientists to dress down. But image is critical. "It's important to appear smart and competent. I wasn't sure if the calendar would hurt my chances for tenure." (He went along with the idea after his girlfriend at the time had sent in the photos.)

Most people think good looks don't hurt. "Generally, looking attractive helps you get a job," Ms. Gallop says. "It's not supposed to be true—and it's nothing that ever gets said— but prejudices operate against people who are seriously over-weight or have bad skin or are really unattractive. It produces a kind of discomfort."

As Ms. Mentor puts it, if A is the cream of the academic crop when it comes to looks, and F is "wolf man," then "wolf man does not get a job." Fortunately, she says, most schol-ars fall somewhere between B+ and D+. But then, she's grad-ing on a curve.

The Pros and Cons of School Dress Codes

Keith A. King

Adults often criticize teen fashion trends as bizarre, indecent, or laughable. Today, however, youth fashions are condemned for more than their appearance. Parents and school faculty have become increasingly concerned over the messages sent by the loose, baggy pants and large T-shirts favored by students—styles inspired by gang clothing. Students as young as elementary school children have been victims of street violence when they were mistaken for gang members after wearing certain colors. Faculty also point out that loose clothing makes it easy to conceal weapons—a very real threat in the modern classroom.

A popular response to such concerns has been the introduction of school dress codes and uniforms. Advocates say uniforms reduce violence in schools because they stop fashion-based competition and the wearing of gang colors and instill a sense of unity among students. Critics, meanwhile, feel that uniforms do not really help the underlying problems that cause violence and undermine students' rights of freedom of expression. Keith A. King, a member of the Department of Health Promotion and Human Performance at the University of Toledo in Ohio, examines both sides of the issue.

■

VIOLENCE AMONG TODAY'S YOUNG PEOPLE, ESPE-cially at school, has been labeled by many health professionals as a potential threat to the overall health and academic success of children. Approximately one in four students reports worrying about becoming a victim of crime or threats at school, and one in eight reports having been victimized at school. In light of such reports, schools have implemented violence prevention programs, which have shown moderate success.

Gang Fashions a Concern

As these programs continue, teachers, principals, parents, and students have also noted a possible connection between school violence and the type of clothing students wear in school. The fashion trend at schools, especially urban schools, is largely dominated by children wearing gang-related or gang-like clothing. The problematic issue of gangs and school violence has been addressed in several studies. With respect to gang-related clothing, gang members frequently roam streets near schools and often enter schools. Hence, the color of clothing that students wear can result in their becoming targets of intentional or unintentional violence. In addition, the style of clothing popular among children today arose from the clothing of inner-city gangs, who have worn baggy pants and oversized shirts that could hide weapons and drugs from law enforcement officials. With such clothing glamorized by music videos and television sitcoms, more children wear similar styles of baggy, oversized shirts and pants to school. Such clothing can become a means of transporting weapons or drugs into school and thus indirectly increase school violence. Add to this the finding that one in three youths reports easy access to handguns, and the concern for school safety becomes especially crucial.

Children's hunger to be fashionable brings another dimension to the connection between clothing style and school violence. Children may envy other children's clothing and lack the financial resources to purchase similar styles. Subsequently, children have been violently injured or even murdered for their designer clothes, sneakers, or professional sport-team paraphernalia. School uniforms may reduce these occurrences. In addition, requiring children to wear the same clothing could send them a message that they all belong to the same team, which may decrease violence toward other "team members."

Uniforms May Reduce Violence

Long Beach (Calif.) Unified School District—comprising 56 elementary schools, 14 middle schools, and nearly 60,000 students—was the first large urban school district in the United States to require school uniforms for all students, kindergarten through grade eight. Since 1994, when mandatory uniform policies were adopted in this school district, district officials have found that violence and discipline problems dramatically decreased. In the first year following implementation, overall school crime decreased by 36%; sex offenses, by 74%; physical fights between students, by 51%; weapons offenses, by 50%; assault and battery offenses, by 34%; school suspensions, by 32%; and vandalism, by 18%.

A proposal calling for mandatory uniforms in elementary schools as a means to reduce youth violence has arisen and has found support among numerous individuals. The President of the United States mentioned the worth of school uniforms in his 1995 State of the Union Address. However, those who oppose the proposal include highly regarded individuals and organizations, the American Civil Liberties Union (ACLU) most notably among them.

The school should provide a safe and disciplined learning environment for students. Violence in schools destroys such an environment and can negatively affect student motivation for learning. Everett and Price found that due to increased prevalence of school violence, one in five public school students feels less eager to go to school every day, one in seven feels less inclined to pay attention to learning in school, and one in 10 stays home from school or cuts class. In unsafe school environments, teachers cannot teach to their maximum potential, and students cannot learn to their full capability.

Youths who feel safe, secure, and free from threats of violence perform better academically. Those who fear for their safety in school or on the way to school may not learn effectively, and they may turn to truancy as a viable alternative to facing the daily threats of violence. One of every 10 to 12 youths who stays away from school does so because of fear. In their response to increasing school violence, several teachers, principals, parents, and students believe uniforms could help reduce violence.

Many Faculty Support Dress Code

Many people believe adoption of school uniform policies will lead to increased school safety, student discipline, and student learning. More specifically, many have argued that school uniforms assist in reducing school violence and theft; preventing gang activity, such as students wearing gang colors and gang insignia; providing discipline in students; helping students to concentrate on their school work; helping students to resist peer pressure; and helping school officials easily recognize school intruders.

In a [1996] survey of the United Teachers of Dade County, Florida, approximately 60% of the group's members supported

Judge Rules in Favor of Dress Code

[In March 2001,] the U.S. Supreme Court declined to hear the appeal of a high school student who was barred from wearing Marilyn Manson T-shirts to school.

The justices declined without comment to hear the appeal of Nicolas J. Boroff, who was a 17-year-old senior at Van Wert High School in Ohio in 1997 when he got into trouble for wearing T-shirts of the Gothic rock group, whose lead singer also performs under the name Marilyn Manson. . . .

Mr. Boroff's appeal argued that Van Wert High administrators had allowed students to wear T-shirts for such heavy-metal groups as Slayer and Megadeth. But when Mr. Boroff showed up in a Marilyn Manson shirt, he was told to remove it, turn it inside out, or go home.

The shirt depicted a three-face image of Jesus Christ with the statement: "See No Truth. Hear No Truth. Speak No Truth." On the back was the word "believe," with the letters "lie" standing out in a different color.

mandatory uniforms for school children. Similarly, of the 5,500 principals surveyed as attendees of the National Association of Secondary School Principals' annual conference in February 1996, more than 70% believed that requiring students to wear uniforms to school would reduce violent incidents and discipline problems. Moreover, greater than 80% of *Long Beach Press-Telegram* readers supported school uniforms.

Some school personnel believe students and teachers tend to behave the way they are allowed to dress. Instead of adopting a policy for mandatory school uniforms, several schools have adopted a mandatory dress code policy for teachers as well as students, which aims to establish clear appearance and behavioral standards for all.

As mentioned previously, Long Beach Unified School District was the first large urban school district in the United States to require school uniforms for all students in grades kinder-

---

Mr. Boroff returned to school three more days wearing different Marilyn Manson T-shirts, and was sent home each time. His mother filed a lawsuit in U.S. District Court in Toledo claiming that the school's actions had violated her son's First Amendment right of free speech. Mr. Boroff never returned to Van Wert High.

The Boroffs lost in the district court and the 6th Circuit court. A panel of the appellate court ruled 2–1 . . . that the school had the authority to prohibit T-shirts that "contain symbols and words that promote values that are so patently contrary to the school's educational mission."

The dissenting judge said it appeared from the evidence that the principal of Van Wert High, William Clifton, had barred the Jesus shirt because it mocked a religious figure. The principal's action could be "viewpoint discrimination," which the First Amendment prohibits, the judge said.

Mark Walsh, "Supreme Court Lets Stand Ruling That Gives Schools Right to Restrict T-Shirts," *Editorial Projects in Education* 20 (28), p. 29, 2001.

garten through grade eight, and it subsequently experienced great decreases in school violence, crime, and negativity. Despite allowing parents the option to request exemption from school uniforms, fewer than 500 parents—less than 1% of all parents—requested exemption in the first year of implementation. Fewer than 400 parents—again, less than 1% of all parents–requested exemption during the 1995–1996 academic year.

Other schools have followed the Long Beach example [including schools in] California, Indiana, Iowa, Louisiana, Massachusetts, Minnesota, New Jersey, Tennessee, Texas, Utah, Virginia, and Washington. [All] have state policies that permit individual schools or districts to adopt school uniform policies or dress codes. Nonetheless, Long Beach Unified and Oakland are the only two school districts to have adopted mandatory uniform policies at the district level. Most school uniform policies are determined at the individual school level. The White House Manual on School Uniforms revealed that several schools with mandatory uniform policies have shown subsequent decreases in school violence and truancy and increases in positive student demeanor.

The Case Against Uniforms

While most parents and teachers seek to ensure the safety and security of their school children, some believe adopting a mandatory school uniform policy is not the appropriate method for ensuring such safety. Two groups opposing mandatory school uniforms are civil libertarians and older students. Loren Siegel, who is director of the ACLU Public Education Department, has stated no one knows for certain whether school uniforms are actually beneficial. While Long Beach Unified School District claims that mandatory school uniforms resulted in decreased school crime and violence, other steps to improve student behavior—such as more teachers patrolling hallways during class changes—were implemented at the same time as the school uniform policy. Due to these possible confounding variables, the ACLU has stated that it is currently impossible to determine whether uniforms were responsible for the results. In addition, no empirical studies show that uniforms consistently produce positive changes in student behavior over time.

The ACLU has also labeled mandatory school uniform policy as not constructive, since such a policy only serves as a "band aid" to a set of serious problems that require multifaceted, multidisciplinary actions. The ACLU stresses that, instead of being directed toward uniforms, resources should be directed toward creating more attractive, clean, and safe school buildings; smaller classes; well-stocked libraries; easily accessed computers; more elective courses, such as music, drama, and art. Such measures could help schools foster long-lasting, positive changes among school children.

Some individuals feel that mandatory school uniforms may teach students a negative lesson about conformity. Some believe that students should base life choices on their own internal values, rather than on rules and regulations arbitrarily set for them, and that this is vitally important to their future health and discipline. Such an argument touches directly upon the rights of freedom of expression for all U.S. citizens. In turn, the ACLU has argued that mandatory uniforms violate students' free expression rights.

Student Reactions

Although most younger children seem to be amenable to uniforms and even like them, many older students, especially adolescents, respond very negatively to school uniforms. One Long Beach seventh grader stated, "It's like we're all in jail." Adolescence is a period when youths attempt to find their own uniqueness and individuality in various ways. One way is through fashion. While many political cartoonists joke that today's youths already wear uniforms of baggy pants, T-shirts, and baseball caps worn backward, these uniforms are acquired by free choice, not enforced by authority figures.

The ACLU conducted a series of focus groups and discussions with high school students to identify what students believed to be solutions to the problem of school violence. School uniforms were not among the solutions students mentioned. Their suggestions did include schools seriously confronting and discussing issues of racial and cultural conflict; providing "safe corridor" programs, which protect student safety to and from school; securing their entrances; providing them more extracurricular activities and clubs; establishing open forums to give them opportunities for self-expression; helping them find part-time jobs; and teaching them conflict resolution skills.

Other Arguments

In October 1995, working on behalf of low-income families, the ACLU of Southern California filed a lawsuit against the Long Beach Unified School District. The lawsuit claimed that the district fails to help low-income students purchase uniforms and has punished students who do not wear them. It also claimed the district does not adequately inform parents about their rights to request exemption from the program. ACLU attorneys assert that low socioeconomic families are going without food, utilities, and rental payments in order to purchase mandatory school uniforms. In response to these claims, Long Beach Unified School officials state that the district has spent more than $100 thousand in donations from individuals and organizations to purchase uniforms and other supplies for financially burdened students. The officials quickly point out that typically, a set of three school uniforms for the year costs between $70 and $90, an amount far less than many students spend for one item of designer clothing.

Another argument against implementing school uniforms involves using student clothing as a barometer for possible personal problems, such as drug use, gang involvement, or sexual abuse. Students' school uniforms may cover up such problems that their clothing might otherwise reveal. In addition, some argue that a mandatory uniform policy tends to penalize everyone as opposed to addressing the children who cause the majority of problems.

Paliokas and Rist noted that for many individuals, the appeal of mandatory school uniforms is based on conventional wisdom and an intuitive belief that increased structure results in improved child behavior. Nevertheless, there is not much empirical data to support a cause-and-effect relationship between school uniforms and violence. Other variables may be intervening with and responsible for possible declines in violence in schools mandating uniforms, and Paliokas and Rist posed several questions that must first be answered before declines in school violence can be specifically attributed to the implementation of school uniform programs. Was the implementation of the uniform policy only one aspect of a comprehensive safety plan that included heightened security and stricter rules? Were local community-policing programs implemented at the same time? Was the trend of violence in the school at its peak and ready to decline? Was there an analysis of the trends of violence within that specific school or school district? Were the decreases in school violence attributed to the Hawthorne Effect in which short-term attention to and visibility of a problem caused the decline? Was parental involvement a crucial factor in the reduction of violence? . . .

Lack of empirical evidence supporting school uniforms does not mean that school uniforms do not work. The following recommendations can assist researchers in examining the effectiveness of school uniforms in preventing and/or reducing school violence:

1) Studies should be conducted which investigate parent, teacher, and student perceptions regarding school uniforms and violence prevention.

2) Studies should use trend analyses to determine whether any decline in violence represents true change or predictable change in trend within the school and/or school district.

3) Studies should statistically control for possible intervening variables associated with violence reduction to determine cause-and-effect relationships between school uniforms and violence reduction.

4) Studies should compare the prevalence of violence in schools mandating uniforms with schools mandating dress codes.

5) Studies should obtain data from both experimental groups (those required to wear uniforms) and control groups (those not required to wear uniforms).

6) Studies should examine how schools mandating uniforms address the issue of providing school uniforms to low-income families.

7) Studies should focus on identifying the means to adequately evaluate the effect of mandatory uniform programs on the prevalence of school violence.

An Economist Looks at the Issue of Clothing Sweatshops

Liza Featherstone and Doug Henwood

New technology and the advent of mass production have greatly affected the American clothing industry. One controversial change has been an increased use of overseas labor. Overseas labor is often much cheaper, in part because American labor laws, which regulate minimum wages and how many hours employees can work, do not protect this alternative workforce. Textile workers in other developing nations are often hired for much less than the minimum wage in the United States. This situation has prompted some American activists—often college students—to protest what they regard as unfair working conditions in so-called sweatshops. Large American clothing manufacturers have been common targets of such criticism; indeed, the word "sweatshop" is nearly synonymous with the mass-market American clothing industry.

The following article focuses on the Workers Rights Consortium (WRC), a student-founded watchdog group, and the Academic Consortium on International Trade (ACIT). While the sweatshop issue has been discussed at length in the press, few articles have addressed the situation from an economist's perspective—the view explored here. Coauthor Liza

■

Excerpted from "Clothes Encounters: Activists and Economists Clash over Sweatshops," by Liza Featherstone and Doug Henwood, *Lingua Franca: The Review of Academic Life*, March 2001.

Featherstone works as a freelance journalist and *Columbia Journal Review* fact checker, while coauthor Doug Henwood edits the *Left Business Observer* and is a contributing editor to the *Nation*.

THE APPEAL FOR BETTER LABOR PRACTICES IN the garment industry did not begin as a campus movement. Throughout the 1990s, labor, left-wing, and religious groups deplored the low wages and harsh conditions prevalent in garment factories throughout the world. Workers in Indonesia and Vietnam, these activists pointed out, often toiled for thirteen hours at a stretch for around twenty cents an hour and in facilities that reeked of toxic fumes. The most prominent anti-sweatshop advocates belonged to the National Labor Committee, whose fiery director, Charles Kernaghan, famously made talk-show personality Kathie Lee Gifford cry on television by revealing that Honduran children worked fifteen hours a day sewing the clothes that bore her label.

Though activists tend to direct their energies at the best-known brands—like Nike, Kathie Lee, Gap, and Reebok—such conditions pervade the apparel industry. (Activists use the word "sweatshops"; companies and most economists reject it as inaccurate and inflammatory.) Garment workers have always been vulnerable to exploitation, partly because the softness of fabric and the complexity of patterns don't allow for easy mechanization. With the decline of international transportation and communication costs since the 1960s, garment manufacturers have increasingly elected to avoid the relatively high wages of U.S. labor by moving most of their factories overseas, often to countries that offer workers little protection. The industry has also become more ruthlessly competitive as increasingly volatile consumer tastes dictate quicker production cycles. In an attempt to keep clothing prices low enough to seduce American teenagers, manufacturers pay the Chinese and Haitian teenagers who make the clothes less than thirty cents an hour.

Student Activism and USAS

Sweatshops are a global issue, but for student activists an obvious target lies close at hand: the hats, sweatshirts, and other items emblazoned with university logos. After a summer internship with the United Needle and Textile Workers Union (UNITE) in 1997, Tico Almeida, then an undergraduate at Duke University, pressed Duke to pass a code of conduct that would require manufacturers of its apparel to maintain safe, independently monitored workplaces in which workers were free to organize. Fellow Duke students were enthusiastic and began lobbying administrators aggressively. They succeeded in getting Duke to enact their code, and the victory inspired students on other campuses to begin similar campaigns.

The next year, Duke students occupied their president's office, demanding that the university go a step further by requiring full disclosure of licensees' factory locations. After a sit-in that lasted thirty-one hours, Duke's president, Nan Keohane, gave in. Similar occupations won students full disclosure at Georgetown, Wisconsin, Michigan, and Chapel Hill. In the spring of 1998, students founded the United Students Against Sweatshops (USAS), a network of campus anti-sweatshop groups, which now has an office in Washington, D.C., and two full-time staff members.

With these successes behind it, the student movement turned to other questions. Codes of conduct were just pieces of paper, the activists realized, unless they were enforced by a credible body. Administrators pointed to the Fair Labor Association (FLA), an industry-backed monitoring group founded by the Clinton administration in 1996, but students scorned it as favoring corporate interests. In fact, several unions and a religious group had resigned from the FLA in 1998, protesting that it relied on voluntary enforcement and set no standard for a living wage. [In 2000], when administrators at many universities, under pressure from garment contractors, insisted on staying with the FLA, students occupied buildings on more than a dozen campuses, including the Universities of Michigan, Wisconsin, Oregon, Pennsylvania, Iowa, and Kentucky, as well as SUNY Albany, Tulane, Purdue, and Macalester. After the tumult subsided, more than fifty institutions had switched to a new monitoring organization founded by students—the Worker Rights Consortium (WRC), which has close ties to local and international labor and human rights organizations. The WRC's membership roster still lags well behind the FLA's 148. (Neither organization has monitored any factories yet.)

The founding of the WRC, which focuses on investigating worker complaints rather than certifying specific companies or factories as "sweat-free," reflects the student movement's increasing emphasis on direct contact with garment workers. Students have visited factories and established relationships with workers throughout Central America and Asia. Critics ranging from the Bangladeshi-born feminist sociologist Naila Kabeer to mainstream pundits like Thomas Friedman have derided First World anti-sweatshop crusades as protectionist, and it's true that a few (though by no means all) of the unions that back the student anti-sweatshop movement can be exactly that. But USAS, which receives funding from the AFL-CIO, has been careful to emphasize that it does not favor banning imports, nor does it call for boycotts. Most apparel workers, USAS activists realize, need their jobs. The goal of the movement is to improve workers' pay and working conditions at offshore factories, not to force universities to take their business elsewhere.

USAS now has chapters on at least 175 campuses, from large state universities to elite East Coast schools to small religious colleges. And although most activists are white and affluent, they are politically diverse. Some embrace anarchism; many passionately resist any form of hierarchy within their organizations. One Penn freshman who participated in a February 2000 sit-in earnestly described himself as a "capitalist"; others, who range from Marxists to Students for a Democratic Society–style radical democrats, denounce capitalism with equal earnestness; still others are liberals with no particular visionary blueprint for the world. Such differences have generally been tolerated, but tensions among these factions broke out at USAS's August 2000 conference in Eugene, Oregon, as activists fought bitterly, even tearfully, over whether the group should create a more centralized, formalized structure or retain its decentralized, loose character.

Faculty Involvement

The members of USAS take their cues more from the labor movement than from the academic left, but the students do have faculty allies, most notably in sociology and cultural studies. The sociologists Edna Bonacich of UC-Riverside and Richard Appelbaum of UC-Santa Barbara, co-authors of *Behind the Label: Inequality in the Los Angeles Apparel Industry* (California, 2000), currently serve on the WRC's advisory council, which assists the students with fund-raising and problem solving. Another sociologist, Peter Dreier, director of Occidental College's Urban & Environmental Policy Program, advises student activists and has taught a seminar on the sweatshop issue. With Occidental activists, Dreier pressed administrators to commission an Occidental T-shirt made by UNITE members in Pennsylvania. Though some activists have criticized this strategy as protectionist, Dreier believes that the union label provides the best available insurance that apparel is "sweat-free."

For all their practical support, many of the professors who advise the students say it's difficult to offer activists much theoretical guidance. One can decry the fact that corporations freely exploit workers and the environment, but these days even intellectuals are hard-pressed to come up with alternative ways to run the world. Some blame the waning of Marxism, whereas others, including Dreier, point to the intellectual dominance of high theory. Dreier complains: "Politics is an entirely theoretical concern for them."

Though it's easy to caricature cultural studies scholars as hopelessly removed from the blood and, yes, sweat of everyday life, some have been quite active in the student movement—not least Andrew Ross, the director of American studies at New York University. Ross edited *No Sweat: Fashion, Free-Trade, and the Rights of Garment Workers,* a collection of essays on the garment industry based on a conference he'd organized called "Fashion Victims." Both book and conference brought together labor activists and cult studs [cultural students] to talk about the rag trade.

Response by Economists

Creative and varied as their approaches have been, however, these professors have not been able to help the students sharpen their economic arguments. There's an obvious reason for this: As Dreier points out, none are economists.

That vacuum looked inviting to [Jagdish] Bhagwati [one of the world's leading trade economists]. Noting that student voices were dominating the sweatshop debate, he saw an opportunity for defenders of free trade to intervene. He drafted a letter criticizing administrators for caving in to activist pressure, worked his Rolodex, and the Academic Consortium on International Trade (ACIT) was born. Bhagwati's draft was worked over by a steering committee that also included Robert Baldwin of Wisconsin, Alan Deardorff and Robert Stern of Michigan, Arvind Panagariya of Maryland, and T.N. Srinivasan of Yale. Of the six, Bhagwati is the most widely known to the general public, because he is a prolific writer of Op-Eds and letters to the editor in newspapers, including the *New York Times* and the *Financial Times*. But all six economists are widely published specialists in international trade, and all have consulted for governments around the world and for international institutions like the World Bank. In addition to its drafters, 246 signatories endorsed the ACIT letter, including the Nobel laureate Robert Lucas of Chicago and Harvard's Jeffrey Sachs. Campuses with active anti-sweatshop campaigns, such as Michigan and Wisconsin, were heavily represented among the signers.

"[W]e often encounter news reports," the professors wrote, "of sit-ins by groups of students in the offices of university/college administrators, after which decisions are often made without seeking the views of scholars in the social sciences, law, and humanities who have long discussed and researched the issues involved." The economists go on to argue that monitoring groups "seem to ignore the well-established fact that multinational corporations (MNCs) commonly pay their workers more on average in comparison to the prevailing market wage for similar workers employed elsewhere in the economy. In cases where subcontracting is involved, workers are generally paid no less than the prevailing market wage." In an interview, Bhagwati told us that the MNC wage premium makes it difficult to argue that Third World apparel workers are "exploited." On the contrary, he says, workers in poor countries feel "lucky" to get jobs with the likes of Nike. They see the work as a "ticket to slightly less impoverishment," he explains with characteristic ambivalence.

The ACIT letter further contends that if activists succeed in driving up wages, "the net result would be shifts in employment that will worsen the collective welfare of the very workers in poor countries who are supposed to be helped." In other words, increasing the cost of labor will reduce the demand for it, so although a few workers might win raises, enough will lose their jobs to make the population as a whole worse off.

During the drafting of the ACIT letter, Bhagwati demurred at the certainty of this last formulation; higher wages could result in layoffs, he says, but "economists are divided" on the likelihood of that happening. The minimum-wage controversy in the United States bears out his caution: For years, economists were certain that minimum-wage increases destroyed jobs, but an empirical study by economists David Card and Alan Krueger, of UC-Berkeley and Princeton respectively, concluded that they didn't, and uncertainty replaced consensus within the profession. But Bhagwati's objection was overruled by the other ACIT drafters, who kept the stronger language in the letter.

Perhaps ACIT's most significant assertion is that MNCs pay better than local firms. The economists are two business school scholars, Ann Harrison of Columbia and Linda Lim of Michigan. Harrison wrote a 1996 paper with Brian Aitken of the International Monetary Fund and Robert Lipsey of the National Bureau of Economic Research that examined wages in the United States, Mexico, and Venezuela. The study concluded that foreign-owned firms pay about 30 percent better than domestic ones, though a significant part of that premium can be explained by the size and nature of MNC plants in countries where few local businesses are comparable. As for Lim, she visited two Nike factories last summer, one in Vietnam and one in Indonesia. In a memo she wrote on her return, Lim noted: "According to the World Bank, the average annual minimum wage for 1995–99 in Vietnam was $134 and the workers at Nike's supplier factory earned $670; in Indonesia the minimum wage was $241 and the workers at the Nike supplier factory earned $720." She cited other studies of Vietnam and Indonesia showing similar results.

Whether or not administrators will be swayed by ACIT's letter remains to be seen. This fall, as students poured their energy into launching the WRC, their battles with administrators temporarily died down. Now they are heating up again, thanks to a strike in a Nike plant in Mexico; ACIT, with its prestigious list of signatories, could become a major player. Administrators at many institutions have reviewed the economists' letter and acknowledged its concerns. At the University of Michigan, president Lee Bollinger has since appointed founding ACIT member Alan Deardorff to the committee that advises administrators on the sweatshop issue. . . .

Living-Wage Studies

[Economist Robert] Pollin first encountered the anti-sweatshop activists in 1999, when students at the University of Wisconsin at Madison invited him to a meeting with the administration convened as part of a settlement package following their sit-in. Pollin's work on living-wage ordinances, which require local governments to do business only with firms that pay their employees more than a specified hourly minimum, had caught the students' attention. Such initiatives are generally opposed by business interests, who—like the ACIT economists—raise the specter of job loss as a bad consequence of the measures' good intentions. Scrutinizing the numbers, Pollin found that both employers and municipal budgets could painlessly withstand a higher-wage bill.

Pollin has since conducted similar studies on sweatshops. Though he hasn't found much good data to work with, his preliminary findings are very similar to his living-wage conclusions: There's plenty of room for substantial wage increases for Third World apparel workers. The best numbers Pollin could find were for Mexico, where wages are higher than those in Asia. A man's casual shirt retailing for $32 in the United States costs $4.74 to produce in Mexico. Of that amount, $0.52 goes to production workers and another $0.52 to supervisors. The retail price, then, is almost seven times the total cost of production and more than thirty times the labor cost alone. You could double the production workers' wage, Pollin argues, and hardly anyone but the workers would be able to tell the difference.

What about the claim that MNCs pay more than local firms? There is plenty of academic ammunition the students might muster to refute the ACIT letter. The Aitken, Harrison, and Lipsey paper focused on Mexico, Venezuela, and the United States. But these are two moderately industrialized, middle-income countries and one highly industrialized, very rich country. Are they comparable with lightly industrialized, poor countries in Asia? As for the Lim study, it draws on anecdotal evidence from Nike plants in only two countries. Even taken together, the two studies form nothing like a systematic wage survey, without which it is dangerous to generalize, given the immense variations in relative pay around the world.

Jeffrey Ballinger, a prominent activist who has interviewed thousands of workers, points out the difficulty of gathering reliable wage data, given government and corporate obstruction of systematic wage surveys. He also questions Lim's focus on annual wages because those figures can include wages for as many as ninety hours of overtime a month.

In any event, mainstream economists may not be asking the only relevant questions. Jeffrey Winters, a Northwestern University professor of political economy who specializes in Southeast Asia, demands, "Should American students be any less outraged just because Nike positions itself slightly higher than some of the exceptionally bad local Indonesian or Vietnamese producers?" Jobs with MNCs "only seem good because prevailing conditions are so horrible." With unemployment and underemployment rates around 50 percent, "Indonesians would line up outside a slave plantation if they could be sure they got regular food and a roof over their heads," says Winters.

The Role of MNCs

Winters suggests using metrics of the sort that most economists regard as otherworldly: "How do wages compare with those of CEOs and celebrity endorsers? What do comparable workers in nonauthoritarian countries where unions are permitted get for comparable work, and under what conditions do they labor? These things matter, even if the Nikes of the world shun these places because they can go to more oppressive locations where nuisances like unions are suppressed." The question MNCs should ask themselves is, he says, "'Can the workers actually live on the wages they earn?' not, 'Is this job better than prostitution, slavery, or starvation?'" The bottom line, Winters concludes, is that "Nike does not pay a living wage and could easily afford to." A company the size of Nike doesn't have to do so on market grounds, but "that's what unions and organizing and protests by students and consumers are all about—it's about injecting very real nonmarket factors into the equation" to maintain "some semblance of humanity."

Pollin concurs. Conceding that MNCs might pay higher wages than local firms, he argues that the real issue is "conditions for all workers." He adds: "The aim should be to change wage norms. We would then be focusing on U.S. companies, since that's where we have relatively greater leverage." More broadly, he explains, "The point of neoliberalism is profit-led growth, with workers getting the shaft. The anti-sweatshop movement is one way of challenging that. But the Linda Lims are quite clever to shift the issue to something else—namely, are conditions at Nike plants worse than at local plants? They know that for the most part they probably are not worse, except maybe with subcontractors. So they can win that argument. But here's another question: Is profit-led growth, where a high fraction if not a huge majority of workers are earning subpoverty wages in bad working conditions, the only way that poor countries can grow? Is it reasonable to give some thought to what might be good for workers, and then also think about how countries might grow in ways that also address those concerns?"

Lim, who was trained as a Marxist economist, dismisses Winters's and Pollin's remarks as "very naive about economics . . . more rhetorical than anything." As for the anti-sweatshop movement, she describes it as "patronizing white-man's-burden stuff." She characterizes the activists' attitudes as, "'let's help these poor Third World women of color who are so victimized by us and are helpless without us,' et cetera— which is just not true and denies the benefit of these jobs to the women. These women aren't dumb, and they do have choices. The 'activists' just don't give enough credit to the women, and to their strength."

Activists Versus Academics

Pollin sees an important role for academics like himself to play in this new battle between activists and mainstream economists. "It's up to the Jeff Ballingers of the world to observe injustice and scream about it," he remarks. "It's then up to us economic sophisticates . . . to try to figure out whether their observations and conclusions make sense. In my view, the collapse of a serious analytic socialist left makes this job all the more difficult. The Bob Sterns and Linda Lims of the world don't get challenged enough by people who can talk their lingo. They know they can win an argument against undergraduates, so they are therefore certain they are right. We need to match their intellectual firepower with some of our own."

As the FLA and the WRC begin their work, there will no doubt be considerable debate about their methods and whether universities and apparel companies are responding properly to their findings. The students are positioning themselves both as a campus protest movement and as part of a new institution, the WRC. In both capacities, they will continue to face assaults from ACIT—and to respond in kind. Now that the progressive economists are getting involved, the fight promises to take on new intellectual dimensions.

Then again, the students could end up finding allies where they least expect them. Bhagwati himself confesses that, the ACIT letter notwithstanding, "I might change my mind about a living wage. And I might then go for WRC!"

When Bhagwati talks about the new generation of activists, he is strangely awestruck. "The kids really, when you see them, they are fierce," he marvels. "They're so fierce—they're carrying these placards, and they're all Down with Corporations! I'm putting the kids on the cover of my next book."

FOR FURTHER RESEARCH

Shari Benstock and Suzanne Ferris, eds., *On Fashion*. Piscataway, NJ: Rutgers University Press, 1994.
This diverse collection, which explores how women's fashions affect—and are affected by—standards of beauty, includes essays about Barbie doll fashions, the impact of Twiggy and Amelia Earhart, and the role of women's magazines in fashion marketing.

Sarah Berry, *Screen Style: Fashion and Femininity in 1930s Hollywood*. Minneapolis: University of Minnesota Press, 2000.
The chapter "Suitably Feminine" provides a good discussion of the influence of movie stars on women's dress reform, while the rest of this book addresses other Hollywood fashion trends such as the impact of exotic styles and consumerism.

Stella Bruzzi, *Undressing Cinema: Clothing and Identity in the Movies*. New York: Routledge, 1997.
This book examines how race, ethnicity, and gender are portrayed in movies through the use of clothing. Chapters include "The Instabilities of the Franco-American Gangster," "The Screen's Fashioning of Blackness," and "The Comedies of Cross-Dressing." A filmography is provided.

Maria Costantino, *Men's Fashion in the Twentieth Century: From Frock Coats to Intelligent Fibres*. New York: Costume and Fashion Press, 1997.
Written from a British perspective, this generously illustrated book offers a chronology of men's clothing styles that includes frequent references to American fashion developments.

Diana Crane, *Fashion and Its Social Agendas: Class, Gender, and Identity in Clothing*. Chicago: University of Chicago Press, 2000.
This anthology contains essays about social issues and fashion both within and outside the United States, including an excellent account of the American women's dress reform movement.

Patricia A. Cunningham and Susan V. Lab, eds., *Dress in American Culture*. Bowling Green, OH: Bowling Green State University Popular Press, 1993.

This collection of nine essays focuses on how American cultural values have influenced fashion.

Jenna Weissman Joselit, *A Perfect Fit: Clothes, Character, and the Promise of America*. New York: Henry Holt, 2001.
Joselit discusses the role of clothing in American culture between 1890 and the 1930s, from men's suits to changing skirt hemlines. The influence of immigrants on American fashion during this period is particularly emphasized.

Angela J. Latham, *Posing a Threat: Flappers, Chorus Girls, and Other Brazen Performers of the American 1920s*. Hanover, NH: Wesleyan University Press, 2000.
Focusing on bathing suits, theater dress, and ladies' balls in 1920s America, Latham provides a detailed overview of associations made at that time between clothing styles, morality, and health.

Library of Congress, *American Memory: Historical Collections for the National Digital Library* [online at http://lcweb2.loc.gov/ammem/]. Washington, DC: Library of Congress, National Digital Library Program, 1994.
Developed and maintained by the Library of Congress, this free searchable online database is an excellent resource with hundreds of historical photographs, drawings, movie stills, and other images of clothing and dress in America. Use *clothing, fashion,* and *dress* as keywords; to find specific references, include relevant terms, such as *clothing and women,* or *Native American dress.*

Alison Lurie, *The Language of Clothes*. New York: Owl Books, 2000.
Recently revised, this landmark book on fashion culture studies is a good introduction to the idea that clothes are not just functional but also a form of personal and cultural expression for gender roles, class, and power.

Ruth P. Rubinstein, *Dress Codes: Meanings and Messages in American Culture*. Boulder, CO: Westview Press, 1995.
In this classic study, Rubinstein demonstrates how clothing is linked to personal and group identity through the use of symbols and dress styles.

Philip Scranton, *Beauty and Business: Commerce, Gender, and Culture in Modern America*. New York: Routledge, 2001.
This collection, which focuses on various aspects of beauty, including hair styles, perfume, body image, and clothing, includes

several chapters on the business of clothing and how retailers and trends influence consumer fashion choices. Essays include "Collars and Consumers: Changing Images of Manliness and Business," "Post-War Beauty Culture and Working Women at Maidenform," and "Negotiating Gender Through Sports Clothing."

George B. Sproles, ed., *Changing Appearances: Understanding Dress in Contemporary Society*. New York: Fairchild, 1994.

This textbook-style anthology of short articles and excerpts is a good starting point for further research, providing a thorough introduction to the popular culture of American fashion, as well as numerous bibliographic references.

Valerie Steele, *The Corset: A Cultural History*. New Haven, CT: Yale University Press, 2001.

Hundreds of illustrations and photographs supplement this broad historical survey, which discusses the popularity and controversies surrounding the corset from several points of view, including designer, consumer, and feminist perspectives.

Tom Vanderbilt, *The Sneaker Book: Anatomy of an Industry and an Icon*. New York: New Press, 1998.

This book focuses on the economic and social aspects of the sport shoe industry and how sneakers have become a part of American popular culture. Extracts from celebrity interviews, fiction, and nonfiction essays about fashion are included.

INDEX